MACMILLAN EXAMS

Ready for

PET

coursebook

Nick Kenny

Anne Kelly

Macmillan Education
Between Towns Road, Oxford OX4 3PP
A division of Macmillan Publishers Limited
Companies and representatives throughout the world

ISBN   978-0-230-02072-6 (without Key)
ISBN   978-0-230-01030-7 (with Key)

First published 2001
This edition 2007

Designed by Jim Evoy
Illustrated by Mike Atkinson; John Dillow; Peter Harper;
Janos Jantner; Ken Harvey; Martin Sanders; David Smith
Cover design by Andrew Oliver

The authors would like to thank Barbara Lewis, David Foll,
Penny Beck, Margaret van Doelen, Nelson Aurich,
Graciela Mazzucco and Russell Crew-Gee for their
help with this book.

The publishers would like to thank the following
consultants and teachers for piloting and reviewing this
book: Andy Hannaford, Anthony Matthews, Barbara Lewis,
Gail Butler, Mabel Turner and Sarah Ellis.

The authors and publishers would like to thank the
following for permission to reproduce copyright material:
University of Cambridge Local Examinations Syndicate for
the answer sheets on pp.92–3.
Adapted extracts from 'Living in the past' by Jerome
Monahan, *The Guardian Education*, 18 July 2000. Copyright
© Jerome Monahan, and reproduced with his permission;
Adapted extracts from 'We crossed a land of ice' by Suzanne
Stevenson, *Metro*, 25 September 2001. Reproduced by
permission of *Metro*; Adapted extracts from 'It's a whale of
a time' by Sarah Tucker, *Travel Metro*, 21 November 2001.
Reproduced by permission of *Metro*; Adapted extracts from
'Idol Pleasures' by Sara O'Reilly, *Time Out London*, 26 June–3
July 2002. Copyright © Time Out Group, and reproduced by
kind permission of Time Out Group. Extract from 'What it
fees like… to win an Oscar' by Adam Jacques copyright ©
The Independent/Adam Jacques 2006, first published in The
Independent on Sunday 26.02.06, reprinted by permission
of the publisher. Extract from 'The Cooking Bus goes round
and round' by Tom Moggach copyright © Guardian
Newspapers Limited 2006, first published in the Guardian
07.02.06, reprinted by permission of the publisher. Extract
from 'Days Out: Dinosaur Isle and Fossil Walk, Isle of Wight'
by Juliet Rix copyright © The Independent/Juliet Rix 2006,
first published in The Independent on Sunday 23.04.06,
reprinted by permission of the publisher. Extract from
'Living in a house felt like prison' by Ros Anderson copyright
© Guardian Newspapers Limited 2006, first published in The
Guardian 15.04.06, reprinted by permission of the publisher.
Extract from 'Heaven on the high seas' by Jenny Cockle
copyright © The Independent/Jenny Cockle 2006, first
published in The Independent on Sunday 19.02.06,
reprinted by permission of the publisher. Extract from 'What
it feels like… to balloon around the world non-stop' by
Richard Middleton copyright © The Independent/Richard
Middleton 2006, first published in The Independent on
Sunday 28.05.06, reprinted by permission of the publisher.
Extract from 'The man who makes children fly' by Maria
Harding copyright © The Telegraph 2006, first published in
The Daily Telegraph 26.04.06, reprinted by permission of the
publisher. Extract from 'To the ends of the earth' by Jenny
Cockle copyright © The Independent/Jenny Cockle 2006,
first published in The Independent on Sunday 07.05.06,
reprinted by permission of the publisher.

The authors and publishers would like to thank the following
for permission to reproduce their photographic material:
Alamy/ Andrew Holt p31(t), Alamy/Adrianko p60;
BananaStock p41(a); Brand X Pictures p49; Corbis/Royalty
Free pp19(t), 57(l), Corbis/David Giles p25(A), Corbis/Michael
Dunn p25(B), Corbis/ Stephanie Colasanti p51;
Empics/William Conran/ PA p31(b); Eye Ubiquitous/Craig
Hutchins pp39(A & B), 48(A), Eye Ubiquitous/Tim Hawkins
p48(B), Eye Ubiquitous/Julia Waterlow p48(C); FLPA/Fred
Bavendam p19(l), FLPA/David Hosking p19(cl), Funday Times
p44; Getty Images/Taxi pp12(A & B), 27, 38, 63(B),
Getty/Stone pp33, 42, 47(B), Getty/Loren Santow p43;
Haddon Davies p54; Image Source p57(r); MHELT pp16(1–5),
28, MHELT/Chris Honeywell p18(A), MHELT/Sue Baker p18(B);
NHPA/Kevin Schafer p19(r); Pathfinder p76(t); PhotoAlto
p76(r); Photodisc pp61, 47(A) Photolibrary/Tui de Roy
p19(cr); Stockbyte pp63(A), 87; SuperStock/age footstock
p6(r), SuperStock/Royalty Free p41(b).

Cover and title page photos
©Thinkstock (ml), ©Digital Vision (l, mr), ©Photodisk (r)

Printed in Thailand

2011   2010 2009   2008 2007
10 9 8 7 6 5 4 3 2 1

With Answer Key

2011   2010 2009   2008
10 9 8 7 6 5 4 3 2

Contents

Introduction

Ready for PET is for students of English who are preparing to take the University of Cambridge Preliminary English Test (PET). *Ready for PET* will get you ready for this test in three important ways. First, it will give you practice in doing the kinds of exercises you will do in the test. Then, it will give you advice on how you can do your best in these exercises. Finally, it will help you learn the vocabulary you need to do the writing and speaking exercises fluently. In this way, you can feel confident about your English when you do the test.

You can use *Ready for PET* in your English class with your teacher, or you can use it to get ready for the test by yourself.

What is the Preliminary English Test (PET)?
The University of Cambridge has tests for students of English at five different levels, from beginners to very advanced students.

PET is at level 2 and is for lower intermediate students. PET tests your reading, writing, listening and speaking. You get 25% of the total marks for the test for each of these four skills. There are three different papers.

Paper 1 is Reading and Writing and takes 1 hour and 30 minutes. In this paper, there are five reading parts and three writing parts. In the reading part of the paper, you have to read some texts and answer some questions on each one. For these questions, you answer by choosing A, B, C or D. In the writing part of the paper, you have to do a short grammar exercise, write a short message, and then write a letter or story. This is a summary of the Reading and Writing paper:

Paper 1: Reading and Writing (1 hour 30 minutes)			
	Type of text	Type of question	Number of questions and marks
Reading			
Part 1	five signs, notices or messages	reading comprehension: multiple choice	5
Part 2	eight short texts	reading comprehension: matching	5
Part 3	one text	reading comprehension: correct/not correct	10
Part 4	one text	reading comprehension: multiple choice	5
Part 5	one text	vocabulary and grammar: multiple choice	10
Writing			
Part 1		grammar	5
Part 2		writing a short message	1 question: 5 marks
Part 3		writing a letter or story	1 question: 15 marks

Paper 2 is Listening and takes about 30 minutes. There are four parts to the paper. You have to listen to a recording and answer some questions. For the questions for three parts, you answer by choosing A, B or C and for one part you write down a few words or numbers. You hear each part of the recording twice. This is a summary of the Listening paper:

Paper 2: Listening (approximately 30 minutes)			
	Type of text	**Type of question**	**Number of questions and marks**
Part 1	seven short recordings (one or two people speaking)	multiple choice pictures	7
Part 2	one or two people speaking	multiple choice	6
Part 3	one person speaking	writing down words	6
Part 4	two people speaking	correct/not correct	6

Paper 3 is Speaking and takes 10–12 minutes. There are four parts to the paper. You do the Speaking test with another student. In the Speaking test, you and your partner talk to an examiner and to each other, while another examiner listens to you. The examiner will ask you some questions and give you some instructions about what you should talk about. In two parts, you have some pictures to talk about. This is a summary of the Speaking paper:

Paper 3: Speaking (10–12 minutes)	
Part 1	The examiner asks you and your partner questions about yourselves.
Part 2	You and your partner look at some pictures showing a situation and talk about it together.
Part 3	You and your partner take it in turns to describe a photograph each.
Part 4	You and your partner have a conversation about the subject (eg holidays) of your photos.

You will find more detailed information about each part of all three papers in the different lessons of *Ready for PET*.

How *Ready for PET* is organized
There are ten units in *Ready for PET* and each unit has two lessons. In each unit, you will find exercises to practise the reading, writing, listening and speaking skills, and the vocabulary and grammar you will need in PET. In each lesson of Units 1–8 there is detailed information and advice about one particular part of the test, and in Units 9–10 you can revise all the advice that has gone before. Throughout the book there are **Get ready** boxes containing clear, helpful exam tips.

At the end of the book there are two PET practice tests. When you do these, you will experience what it is like taking the real test. You will see how much time you have to do each question and you will find out which parts of the test you need to practise more.

The **CD-ROM** which comes with the book has six Reading, Writing and Listening tests. These tests provide extensive practice of PET test tasks.

When you've worked through *Ready for PET*, you'll know what to expect in every part of the test, and you'll have the language you need to do the test well.

For students studying alone

If you are preparing for PET without a teacher, *Ready for PET* will help you. You should use *Ready for PET* at the same time as your general English coursebook. Your coursebook will develop your knowledge of English, and *Ready for PET* will give you the special practice you need for the test exercises.

Remember to use the 'with key' edition of *Ready for PET,* which has a key to exercises and recording scripts of the listening texts at the back. When you have finished each exercise, check your answers with the key. Don't look at the key until you have done each exercise. If necessary, you can use a dictionary to help you with unknown words, but always try to guess the meaning of words first. You should also see if you can answer the questions without knowing the difficult words.

The texts of the listening exercises are on a CD. In the PET Listening test, you hear each listening text twice, so when you are practising with these exercises, listen twice before checking your answers. If you don't understand something you can look at the recording script, but never do this until you have listened to the recording twice.

There are many writing exercises in *Ready for PET*. It's useful if you can ask a teacher to correct these for you, but it doesn't matter if this isn't possible. Just doing the writing is good practice. Always make sure you follow the instructions exactly and check your own work carefully.

There are also many speaking exercises in the book. It's difficult to do speaking exercises if you're studying alone, but it's important that you get speaking practice. Remember, 25% of the marks for the whole of PET are for the Speaking test, so if possible, do the speaking exercises with another student. If you can't do this, do the exercises by yourself and record what you say. Then listen to yourself speaking and think of ways in which you could do the exercise better. Don't worry about making mistakes, but try to express your ideas clearly.

On pages 66–87, there are two practice tests. You should try to do at least one of these like a real test. Only take the amount of time allowed for the test, and do it without any dictionary or notes to help you.

You can also use the CD-ROM to give yourself practice doing PET Reading, Writing and Listening tasks. There are six tests on the CD-ROM. Do a test at regular intervals while you are studying. Check your answers and keep a record of your scores to get an idea of the progress you are making.

Before you start, decide how many hours a week you can spend studying with *Ready for PET* and keep to this decision. It is better to study regularly for short periods than to try and do everything just before the day of the test.

The PET preparation diary on the opposite page will help you to organize your study. Fill in the date you start your PET preparation at the top, and the date you will take PET at the bottom. Then work out how many days or weeks you have to complete each unit of this book. When you have completed a unit, write the date in the space provided, and decide how well you have done in the different practice exercises in that unit (self-assessment). In the 'Study notes' section you can write anything which will help you. For example, you may want to make a note of some exercises you want to look at again, or some exercises which you haven't had time to do and plan to work on later. You can also keep a record of the scores you get on the CD-ROM Practice tests. You should organize your study in the way which best suits you in the time you have available before you take PET.

PET preparation diary			
I began preparing for PET on: (date)			
Unit	Study notes	Self-assessment ✔ = I did well ✘ = I need more practice	CD-ROM Practice tests
1 completed on		Reading Listening Speaking Writing Vocabulary	**Practice test 1** Date .... Total Reading score .... Total Listening score ....
2 completed on		Reading Listening Speaking Writing Vocabulary	**Practice test 2** Date .... Total Reading score .... Total Listening score ....
3 completed on		Reading Listening Speaking Writing Vocabulary	
4 completed on		Reading Listening Speaking Writing Vocabulary	**Practice test 3** Date .... Total Reading score .... Total Listening score ....
5 completed on		Reading Listening Speaking Writing Vocabulary	
6 completed on		Reading Listening Speaking Writing Vocabulary	**Practice test 4** Date .... Total Reading score .... Total Listening score ....
7 completed on		Reading Listening Speaking Writing Vocabulary	
8 completed on		Reading Listening Speaking Writing Vocabulary	**Practice test 5** Date .... Total Reading score .... Total Listening score ....
9 completed on		Reading Speaking Writing Vocabulary	
10 completed on		Reading Listening Speaking Writing Vocabulary	**Practice test 6** Date .... Total Reading score .... Total Listening score ....
I am taking PET on: (test date)			

Personal information

1 Writing

Complete this form with information about yourself.

SIGN UP NOW!

Name:

Surname:

Home town:

E-mail address:

Mobile number:

Sex: Age:

Interests:

2 Listening 1.1   **1 Listen to two people talking about themselves and fill in the missing information.**

SIGN UP NOW!

Name:

Surname:

Home town:

E-mail address:

Mobile number:

Sex: Age:

Interests:

A

SIGN UP NOW!

Name:

Surname:

Home town:

E-mail address:

Mobile number:

Sex: Age:

Interests:

B

2 If you wanted to find out more information about these people, what questions would you ask? Make questions beginning with each of these words.

Are ... ?

When ... ?

What ... ?

Do ... ?

Where ... ?

How ... ?

3 Speaking

1 Look at the activities in the box. Which of these activities are you good at? Order the activities from most interesting (1) to least interesting (12).

Talk about why you like (1) and why you dislike (12).

watching sports	playing sports	computer games
watersports	collecting things	playing a musical instrument
dancing	learning languages	making things
driving	keep-fit exercises	surfing the Internet

2 How do you spell your name? Practise saying the letters in English.

1.2 3 Listen to five people spelling their names. Write their names below:
1 .... 2 .... 3 ....
4 .... 5 ....

Talk to the examiner.

Answer the questions!

Make your answers interesting!

Get ready for PET Speaking Part 1

1 In Part 1 of the Speaking Test, the examiner asks you questions. Be ready to talk about:
- your home and family
- what you do every day
- your work and studies
- your likes and dislikes

2 When you answer, remember to:
- say what you really think
- answer the questions directly
- say why – give reasons and examples
- make the conversation interesting
- talk to the examiner, not to your partner

3 The examiner also asks you to spell your name.
- Practise spelling all parts of your name.
- Make sure you can do it perfectly.
- Make sure you can do it at normal speed.

4 Writing

Complete the second sentence so that it means the same as the first, using no more than three words.

1 Do you play football well?
   Are you a .... player?

2 Do watersports interest you?
   Are you .... watersports?

3 What is your age?
   How .... you?

4 Which is your favourite school subject?
   Which school subject .... like best?

5 How is your surname spelt?
   How do .... your surname?

5 Writing

You have decided to join an English-language club on the Internet. Write a brief description of yourself for the database. You can write up to 100 words. Remember to include:

- your personal details, for example, name and age
- what you do/study
- the things that you are interested in

6 **Listening**

1 **David and Victoria have just met at a party. Complete the gaps in their conversation using the phrases below. Write the correct letters in the spaces.**

David: Hello. I'm David.

Victoria: **(1)** ....

David: Yes, I'm one of his friends too, and we play football together. What do you study?

Victoria: **(2)** ....

David: I've finished college, actually, and I'm working as a windsurfing instructor.

Victoria: **(3)** ....

David: That doesn't matter. You could learn.

Victoria: **(4)** ....

David: So am I. I'm running a course which starts next week. Would you be interested in joining?

Victoria: **(5)** ....

Use five of these phrases to complete Victoria's part of the conversation.

A English. Have you finished college?

B Yes, I suppose so. But what I'm really interested in is sailing.

C Hi. I'm Victoria. I'm a friend of Tom's from college.

D Hello, I'm Victoria. I'm really interested in football.

E I'm doing languages. What about you?

F Oh, I'm really interested in watersports, but I'm not very good at windsurfing.

G Oh … I might be … it depends.

1.3 **2** **Which two didn't you use? Now listen and check.**

3 **When you meet someone of your own age for the first time:**

• what questions do you ask them?

• what are good things to talk about?

• what do you tell them about yourself?

7 **Reading**

1 **Look at these notices and choose the correct explanation, A, B or C.**

This notice is telling you   1

A what information to write.

B which type of letters to use.

C which type of pen to use.

> Please write in
> BLOCK CAPITALS

This notice is giving you   2

A some advice.

B a suggestion.

C an instruction.

> **ALL PACKAGES
> MUST BE
> SIGNED FOR**

2 **What is a signature? How is it different from other ways of writing your name? Write your name in block capitals:** ....

Write your signature: ....

A regular thing

1 Match the words in A with the words in B. For example, *comb* and *hair* go together. Some words are used more than once.

A

attend	boil	brush	clean	comb
dial	dust	feed	iron	miss
tidy	tie	wash		

B

bus	class	desk	dishes
furniture	hair	meeting	number
pet	shirt	shoes	
shoelaces	teeth	water	

Which of these things do you do regularly, sometimes, occasionally or never? Talk about some of your habits using the words in the boxes.

2 Now match the words in C with the words in D. Some words are used more than once.

C

hand in	join in	take off
put on	put up	put away
turn up	plug in	turn on

D

books	game	homework
make-up	music	radio
socks	umbrella	light

Use the words in the boxes to talk about your daily life.

What kinds of short message do you write to people in your daily life?
Read these short messages.

A

Mum,
All my white sports shirts are
dirty! I must wear a clean one in
the tennis match tomorrow. Could
you wash and iron one for me? If
you can, I'll wash up after dinner
every night for a week! Thanks a lot.
Julia

B

E-mail:

....

To: Paulo
From: Emilio

....

Thanks for telling me about
the English homework. I'm
worried I won't be able to do
it because I missed the
lesson. Why don't you come to
my house on Saturday and we
can do the exercises together?

C

P O S T C A

Dear Gemma,
My cousin Lou and I visited Brighton yesterday.
What a pity you couldn't come with us! We went
shopping, and then we visited a beautiful old palace
called Brighton Pavilion. My favourite part of the
day was eating ice cream on the beach.
Love, Jodie

In which message (or messages), is the writer

1 thanking someone for something?
2 describing what s/he has done?
3 explaining why s/he needs to have something?
4 telling someone what s/he liked best about something?
5 asking someone to do something for him/her?
6 saying how s/he feels about something?
7 suggesting an activity?
8 offering to do something?

3 Writing

1 Imagine this situation and then write a short message to a classmate.
You want to ask a classmate to help you do something.
Write a note to your classmate. In your note, you should

- explain what help you'd like your classmate to give you
- suggest a time when your classmate can help you
- offer to do something for your classmate

Write 35–45 words.

2 Read your classmate's note to you and then write another note in reply.
In your note, you should

- agree to help your classmate
- suggest a *different* time to give this help
- accept your classmate's offer

Remember to write something about each point – that's three things to write.

Write 35–45 words.

Get ready for PET Writing Part 2

1 The first line of the instructions describes a situation to you. Read this carefully and imagine the situation.
2 The instructions tell you to write *three* points in your message. Make sure you say something about each point.
3 Remember to address your message to the person named in the instructions (eg *Dear Alice, Hi Ben*).

4 Don't forget to write your name at the end of your message.
5 Don't write fewer than 35 words or more than 45 words.
6 Check what you have written.

3 Write one of these short messages.
Your English friend, Alice, helped you with your English homework last week.
Write a card to send to Alice. In your card, you should

- thank Alice
- tell her what your teacher said about your homework
- suggest when you could see Alice again

Remember to write 'Dear Alice' and to sign your card.

Write 35–45 words.

You took a phone call for your English friend, Ben, about a parcel.
Write the phone message for Ben. In your message, you should

- tell Ben who phoned
- say what is in the parcel
- explain what Ben should do when the parcel arrives

Remember to check what you have written.

Write 35–45 words.

4 Writing

There are several ways to make comparisons.
Examples:

*Sam listens to the radio **more** often **than** Marcia does.*
*Marcia listens to the radio **less** often **than** Sam does.*
*Marcia doesn't listen to the radio **as** often **as** Sam does.*

*My shoes are clean**er than** my brother's.*
*My brother's shoes are dirt**ier than** mine.*
*My brother's shoes aren't **as** clean **as** mine.*

*My grandmother is **better** at ironing **than** my mother.*
*My mother is not **as** good at ironing **as** my grandmother.*
*My mother is **worse** at ironing **than** my grandmother.*

Complete the second sentence so that it means the same as the first, using no more than three words.

1 Your bedroom is tidier than mine.
   My bedroom isn't .... yours.
2 Gerry doesn't do the washing-up as fast as Paul.
   Paul does the washing-up .... Gerry.
3 The new armchair isn't nearly as comfortable as the old one.
   The old armchair is much .... the new one.
4 Every evening, Sally does a lot more homework than Rachel.
   Every evening, Rachel does a lot .... Sally.
5 This music isn't nearly as bad as the music they play on Radio 2.
   The music they play on Radio 2 is far .... this music.

---

5 Reading

1 **What inventions of the last 2,000 years have caused the most important changes in people's daily lives?**

2 **Read this text and choose the correct word, A, B, C or D for each space.**

INVENTIONS OF THE LAST 2,000 YEARS

Recently, hundreds of scientists and philosophers were asked to name the most important invention of the last 2,000 years. You might **(1)** .... people to say the Internet, penicillin or the internal combustion engine, but in **(2)** .... nobody did. One scientist **(3)** .... for paper because, long before the Internet, paper allowed ideas to be sent around the world. **(4)** .... scientists agreed that modern medicine has helped millions of people, but said **(5)** .... inventions, such as soap and pipes for clean and dirty water, have **(6)** .... more lives. One philosopher said hay was the most important because it's winter food for horses. Without **(7)** ...., horses couldn't exist in cold climates, **(8)** .... meant that there couldn't be cities in places colder than Athens and Rome. So, thanks **(9)** .... hay, Vienna, Paris, London and Berlin were built! Someone else named the mirror because in **(10)** .... at our own faces we can learn about human beings in general.

1	A expect	B think	C believe	D guess
2	A all	B fact	C particular	D detail
3	A suggested	B judged	C answered	D voted
4	A Other	B Another	C Others	D Any
5	A clearer	B plainer	C simpler	D purer
6	A rescued	B delivered	C saved	D recovered
7	A them	B it	C these	D many
8	A what	B that	C where	D which
9	A to	B of	C by	D from
10	A seeing	B looking	C watching	D studying

2 ① You live and learn

1 Look at the photographs.

A

B

In which of the photos can you see these things?

mouse	screen	desk
blackboard	keyboard	pen
chair	map	

somebody ...	asking	thinking
	talking	reading
	explaining	waiting

2 What other things can you see in the photographs?

2 Speaking

1 Look at these ideas. Which five do you think are the best ways to learn English?

surfing the Internet
studying a textbook
going to classes
playing computer games
doing grammar exercises

?

listening to songs
watching satellite TV
talking to people in English
watching films in English
reading newspapers and magazines

🎧 1.4 **2** Listen to Polly. She is studying Spanish.

- Which is her favourite way of studying Spanish?
- Choose the correct picture.

A ☐   B ☐   C ☐

- Why does Polly like studying in this way?

3 You want to ask Polly about the things in the box below. Write the questions.

the teacher	length of each class	number of students
the book(s) and equipment	type of people	cost of course
the classroom	number of classes per week	what she's learnt

---

3 Speaking

1 Look at this situation.

A young friend of yours wants to learn a new language in his free time.
He has a small amount of money to spend on this new hobby.
First talk about the things he can buy to help him learn the language.
Then say which will be the best use of his money.

Talk to your partner.

Talk about the situation — not about yourself!

Say what you think — explain why.

Ask for your partner's opinions.

Look at these ways of starting the discussion.
Where shall we begin?
Let's talk about x first.
How about ..., what do you think of that idea?

Look at these ways of saying what you think.
I think ... is a good idea because ...
I think ... is better than ... because ...
I think s/he should buy ... because ...
I think the best thing (for him/her) to buy is ... because ...

Look at these ways of responding to what your partner says.
That's a good idea because ...
I'm not so sure about that because ...
And what do you think about ...?

Get ready for PET Speaking Part 2

1 Listen to the instructions. Are you talking about yourself or somebody else?
2 Speak to your partner, not to the examiner.
3 Remember to *listen* to your partner and *respond* to what s/he says.
4 Say *what* you think and explain *why* you think it.

2 **Pietro and Valerie are doing exercise 3.1. Complete the gaps in their conversation using the phrases below. Write the correct letters in the spaces.**

Valerie: So, our friend wants to learn a new language?
Pietro: **(1)** ....
Valerie: No, he can't. Let's start by talking about which of them will be useful for him.
Pietro: **(2)** ....
Valerie: OK. Shall we start with this one, the dictionary?
Pietro: **(3)** ....
Valerie: Yes, I agree, and it's also good for checking spelling. But what about a textbook? They're useful too.
Pietro: **(4)** ....
Valerie: Possibly. Or he may get one free when he pays for the course.
Pietro: **(5)** ....

Use five of these phrases to complete Pietro's part of the conversation.

A Oh yes, that's a good point.
B I don't like them very much.
C Yes they are, but maybe he won't need one because he'll have a teacher.
D Would you like a dictionary or a textbook?
E OK, then afterwards we can decide which one he should buy.
F That's right, and he's only got £20 to spend, so he can't buy all these things, can he?
G Yes, I think he should buy one of those, because it's very useful if you don't know what words mean.

🔊 1.5 **3** **Which two phrases didn't you use? Now listen and check.**

4 Listening 🔊 1.6
- Look at these five sentences.
- Listen to Tim and Janet talking about the courses they are doing in their free time.
- Decide if each sentence is correct or incorrect.
- If you think it is correct, put a tick (✓) in the box under **A** for **YES**. If you think it is not correct, put a tick (✓) in the box under **B** for **No**.

		A YES	B No
1	Janet thinks her computer classes are too long.	☐	☐
2	Tim has learnt many new things on his course.	☐	☐
3	Tim has to buy the food he cooks on his course.	☐	☐
4	Tim asks Janet to help him with his cookery.	☐	☐
5	Janet agrees to help Tim solve a problem.	☐	☐

5 Writing

Complete the second sentence so that it means the same as the first, using no more than three words.

1 Each lesson lasts two hours.
Each lesson .... long.

2 What's the price of this CD-ROM, please?
How .... this CD-ROM cost, please?

3 I think a dictionary is very useful.
A dictionary is very useful .... opinion.

4 I think you are right about the textbook.
I agree .... you about the textbook.

5 Let's talk about the videotape first.
How .... about the videotape first?

1 Reading

Read the notices and answer the questions.
- Which one can you probably see in **a)** a library? **b)** a bookshop?
- Which one is **a)** advertising something? **b)** warning you?
- What does each notice mean? Choose **A, B** or **C**.

1

Just published

**Mediterranean Cookery
by Poppy Tobin**

Signed copies available on request

A We have published all of Poppy Tobin's books about cooking.

B Sign here if you'd like a copy of Poppy Tobin's latest book.

C Buy a new book with the writer's signature in it here.

2

Please respect all books in your care.

Heavy fines for any damage to borrowed books.

A Take care when looking at damaged books.

B You'll have to pay if you don't look after our books.

C You can use these books here, but you can't borrow them.

2 Vocabulary

Look at these book covers. What type of book do you think each one is? Choose your answers from the words in the box.

| mystery | romance | horror | science fiction |
| thriller | biography | humour | travel |

Which of these books would you like to read? Why do you enjoy this type of book?

A B C D

E F G H

3 Reading

The people in 1–5 all want to buy a book.
- Look at the descriptions of eight books (A–H).
- Decide which one would be most suitable for each person.

1 Laura is looking for a book for her grandson's fifth birthday present. Preferably, it should be about space travel or animals and be a story she can read to him many times.

2 Moira's 14-year-old daughter loves science fiction videos. Moira wants to encourage her to read more by giving her a book which will hold her attention.

Underline the words that describe what is important for each person. Only ONE book will match ALL these details.

3 Fiona, like everyone in her family, is very interested in the cinema and enjoys reading about it. She wants a book that will give her all the gossip about film stars past and present.

4 James, who is 15, is looking for something to pass the time on a long plane journey. He'd like to read an adventure story which brings a period of history to life.

5 Gerry likes mystery stories which are full of suspense and excitement. He'd prefer to buy a book by a new writer.

This week's bargain books

A The Meeting
This exciting novel is aimed at teenagers but adults will enjoy it, too. It's the 16th century and Per, the farm boy, rescues a princess. There are marvellous chases, battle scenes and romantic meetings – you couldn't ask for more thrilling action in a story, or a more realistic picture of the past.

B Stealing Scenes
Starting at the age of five, the writer of this amusing autobiography has had a long and successful career as an actress on stage and screen. She takes us into her world of lights and cameras and tells the secrets of famous people she has known.

C The Bucketful of Dinosaurs
When Harry finds a bucketful of dinosaurs, he's delighted and takes them everywhere he goes until one day he leaves them on a train. How will he prove that the dinosaurs belong to him? Very young children will never get tired of listening to this charming adventure.

D Blood Rain
In this seventh book in the series about an Italian police inspector, the hero investigates a murder. The victim? Maybe just a friendless nobody, or perhaps the son of the country's most powerful criminal. Can the inspector manage both to find the murderer and to stay alive?

E Hex Shadows
This story is set in the year 2367 when Britain is a part of the cruel European Federation. Hexes, human computers who were created in the late 21st century, are now hunted down as enemies of the Federation. This is an exciting, fast-moving story which teenagers will love.

F Space Age
Designed with the fact-hungry child in mind, this gives information about stars, galaxies, astronauts and spaceships. It will bring the universe to life and make science and technology fun for those between five and ten years old.

G Stormy Weather
This thriller is the first from the pen of a young Canadian. It follows the story of Dale, a meteorologist who is invited on a small plane to watch a thunderstorm. Dale soon discovers that not all dangers come from nature, and to save his life he must find the answers to some deadly questions.

H Shoot!
For more than 20 years, this has been recognized as the best guide to the movies. This latest edition gives details and opinions about more than 22,000 films. It tells you about video and DVD availability, which films are suitable for family viewing, and the prizes films have won.

Get ready for PET Reading Part 2

1 Look at the information about Laura. Underline the words that are important about her.
Have you underlined: *grandson's fifth birthday, space travel or animals* and *read ... many times*?

2 Which book would be suitable for a child of five (*grandson's fifth birthday*)? Are A, B or E suitable? Why not?
What about C and F? Why? (*very young children, those between five and ten years old*)

3 Are C and F about *space travel* or *animals*? Remember, dinosaurs are animals.

4 C and F can't both be suitable. Which one is unsuitable? Why? So which is the most suitable book for Laura?

5 Now do the same for the other people.

---

4 Vocabulary

Harry had a *bucketful* of dinosaurs. Complete these sentences in an interesting way.

1 Brian can't speak because he's just taken a mouthful of ....

2 You won't get better unless you swallow this spoonful of ....

3 When nobody was looking, Katia gave me a handful of ....

4 Graham felt hungry when he looked at the plateful of ....

5 Jenny's jacket was heavy because she had a pocketful of ....

5 Writing

1 This is a story called 'The Strange Visitor'. The sentences aren't in the right order. Read the sentences and put them in the correct order. The first one has been done for you.

☐ She knew what she had to do.

☐ Jenny cried out in surprise and the strange visitor disappeared.

☐ Although the person didn't speak, Jenny could hear some words in her head.

[7] One day when Jenny arrived home, she saw someone standing at her front door, hidden underneath a large, old-fashioned coat and hat.

☐ To prepare for that day, you must study hard and learn all you can.'

☐ She went inside, took out her homework and studied all evening.

☐ She didn't know why, but she felt that this person was very old, wise and kind.

☐ 'This is only my first visit, and when we meet again I will show you my home on a distant planet.

2 Now you are going to write your own story. It is also called 'The Strange Visitor', but it must be a *different* story.

Before you start to write, answer these questions about your own story.

• Who does the visitor come to see?

• Where and when does the visit happen?

• What is strange about the visitor?

• How does the person visited feel about the visitor?

• What happens in the end?

3 Write your story in about 100 words.

3 ① Holiday adventures

1 Reading

Read these notices. Which one can you see a) in a travel agency window? b) at an airport? c) in a hotel?

1

Find out about excursions, nightlife and transport to the airport at our 24-hour reception desk

2

70,000 package holidays
Reservations 9 am – 6 pm

Leave an answerphone message outside these hours

3

Do not leave your luggage unattended at any time

What does each notice mean? Choose A, B or C.

A Make sure there's always someone with your belongings.

B You can make a booking here during the day.

C Someone is always available to give you information.

2 Speaking

1 Look at picture A and answer these questions. Use the words in the box.
1 Who can you see in the picture?
2 Where is she?
3 What's she doing?
4 What things can you see in the picture?
5 How does the girl probably feel? Why?

suitcase	young	wearing	packing
bedroom	nervous	clothes	holiday
quilt	abroad	plastic	woman

A

2 Now use your answers to describe the picture.
Begin: *This picture shows a young woman in her bedroom. She's …*

3 Now look at picture B. Describe what you can see in the picture. Talk about:
• where the picture was taken
• the people
• what they are doing
• the things you can see
• what they are probably talking about

Use these words:

jacket	phone	writing
curly	arrangements	brochures
discussing	travel agency	shelf
desk	trip	pen

B

Begin: *This picture shows two people in a travel agency. They're …*

3 Reading

Don't worry if you don't understand some words.

Do the sentences match what the text says?

1 Would you like to go on an adventure holiday? Read about a scuba-diving boat tour to see if it could be the holiday for you.

2 Read the text to decide if each sentence is correct or incorrect.

1 The giant tortoises in the Galapagos Islands are over 120 years old.
2 The Galapagos penguins live further north than any other penguins.
3 You can always be sure of seeing whales in the Galapagos.
4 There's so much to see in the Galapagos that you should stay at least seven days.
5 Divers get the chance to go walking on Darwin Island.
6 It's safe to go looking for sharks round Wolf Rocks if you're new to diving.
7 On the boats, passengers have sleeping accommodation on two different levels.
8 Each boat has a total of five members of staff.
9 If you like, you can go to the Andes after you've finished diving in the Galapagos.
10 You can use the Internet to book a holiday in the Galapagos.

Go on a scuba-diving holiday in the Galapagos Islands on a *Scuba Tours* dive boat and explore a fascinating sea and land environment.

The Galapagos Islands

These extraordinary islands lie in the Pacific Ocean, 1,000 kilometres off the coast of Ecuador. Some of the world's strangest creatures live here, for example giant tortoises that can reach 120 years in age and marine iguanas that look like prehistoric dinosaurs. The Galapagos are also home to penguins (nowhere else are they found so far north) and sea ea lions. Underwater it is a paradise for divers and snorkellers. A flow of cold water from the south meets a flow of warm water from the north, meaning it is possible to find a huge range of sea life. Hammerhead sharks suddenly appear out of nowhere, and, at certain times of year, whales pass by the islands. The wildlife and scenery is so varied here that a seven-day voyage is the minimum you should consider, and we recommend 14 days to get the most from the experience.

Diving opportunities

Our tour starts at San Cristobal and we travel northwards, past North Seymour Island to Wolf and Darwin Islands. This route offers some of the most spectacular diving opportunities in the world. There are three or four dives every day and one or two land tours, except at Wolf and Darwin as landing there is forbidden. Divers usually mention visits to Mosquera (for the sea lions) and Bartolome (for the penguins) as highlights. Wolf Rocks is a favourite place to see sharks, though this site is not suitable for inexperienced divers.

The accommodation

Scuba Tours has two boats, Sea Bird and Sea Wind. Each boat is 30 metres in length and has four levels. On the lowest level, there are four cabins to accommodate eight people. Above this is the main deck where there is a comfortable sitting and dining area. On the upper deck, there are three more double cabins, and above this an open-air sun deck. A crew of five look after you on board, and a further four crew members take care of you when you are in the water or on land tours.

Additional land tours

On request, we can arrange a variety of additional land tours on the mainland of Ecuador. These tours include four days in the Amazon rainforest, a visit to volcanoes in the Andes mountains, and trips to some fascinating markets. Apart from the Amazon tour, which has fixed departure dates, these can be added at the start or end of any Galapagos diving holiday.

Prices and booking

For current prices and an online reservation form, visit our website at www.scubatours.com.

4 Writing

There are several ways to say *when* something happens.
Examples:
*You must get a scuba-diving certificate **before** you can go on a diving holiday.*
*You can go on a diving holiday **after** you have got a scuba-diving certificate.*
*You can't go on a diving holiday **until** you have got a scuba-diving certificate.*

***When** the divers reached Wolf Rocks they saw some sharks.*
*The divers saw some sharks **as soon as** they reached Wolf Rocks.*

*People make a lot of new friends **while** they're on a scuba-diving holiday.*
*People make a lot of new friends **during** a scuba-diving holiday.*

Complete the second sentence so that it means the same as the first, using no more than three words.

1 Learn to ski before you go on a winter holiday in the mountains.
Don't go on a winter holiday in the mountains until .... to ski.

2 When we arrived at the hotel, we immediately went for a swim.
We went for a swim as .... we arrived at the hotel.

3 We'll go sightseeing after lunch.
We'll go sightseeing when .... had lunch.

4 During my holiday in Paris, I spoke a lot of French.
I spoke a lot of French while I .... in Paris.

5 Don't book your holiday until you've seen my photos of Africa.
You must see my photos of Africa .... your holiday.

5 Vocabulary

You can use the words in the box when you're talking about holidays. Divide them into the six groups.

hotel countryside
sunglasses shells
plane taking photos
swimming coach
postcards train
guest house car
sunbathing tent
suntan lotion
handicrafts beach
guidebook picnics

Transport	Accommodation	Scenery	Activities	Things to pack	Souvenirs
car	hotel	beach	swimming	sunglasses	postcards

Think of words which describe the kind of holiday you like most. Use a dictionary to help you. Add the words to the table.

6 Speaking

Talk about the kind of holidays you like and don't like.

1 Reading

Read these messages. What does each one say? Choose A, B or C.

1

```
E-mail:
..................................................
To:    Ronan
From:  David
..................................................
Several members of staff are
wearing jeans with their
uniform jackets, which they
know is against company
rules. Can you speak to
them? Thanks.
```

The boss wants Ronan to

A inform staff about new company rules.

B ask staff for their opinion of the company uniform.

C warn staff their appearance isn't satisfactory.

2

Ronan,

During the bus strike next week, I can give you a lift to the office. Shall I pick you up at 7 o'clock?

Maddy

What is Maddy offering to do for Ronan?

A drive him to work

B wake him up early

C accompany him on the bus

Do you think Ronan will be happy to receive these messages? What kinds of things make people happy or unhappy at work?

2 Vocabulary

1 Many people have to study for several years before they take up a profession or job. For example, an *architect* has studied *architecture*, and a *doctor* has studied *medicine*. What have these people studied?

Profession	Subject studied
architect	*architecture*
doctor	*medicine*
lawyer	
artist	
cook	
engineer	
tourist guide	
hairdresser	
journalist	
businesswoman	
actor	
chemist	
biologist	
physicist	
musician	

2 Look at these verbs. You can make nouns by changing the end of each one. Complete the table.

Verb	Noun
apply	*application*
organize	
qualify	
decide	
operate	
employ	*employment*
advertise	
govern	
manage	
retire	
insure	
succeed	

Use the pairs of words to make sentences.
Example:
If you want to apply for a job, you have to fill in an application form.

3 **Listening** 🔊 1.7–10 **1** You will hear four women talking about their jobs. Listen and complete the information in the table.

Speaker	Clothes	Equipment	Place	Activity
1				*controlling traffic*
2			*advertising agency*	
3		*microscope*		
4				

Listen again and match the speakers with the pictures, **A**, **B**, **C** or **D**.

A

B

C

D

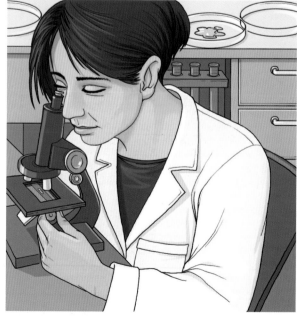

3 Listening 🔊 1.11 **2 You will hear a woman talking on the radio about her job. Put a tick (✓) in the correct box for each question.**

Read all the questions quickly first.

1 Where does Amanda usually work?
- A ☐ in a restaurant
- B ☐ in her own kitchen
- C ☐ in recording studios

Be ready to listen for the answer to the next question even if you have missed the answer to the first one.

2 People are satisfied with Amanda's service because
- A ☐ she provides large meals.
- B ☐ she cooks healthy food.
- C ☐ she prepares unusual dishes.

3 Amanda finds her job stressful if she
- A ☐ has to work in unsuitable places.
- B ☐ doesn't know when she should serve a meal.
- C ☐ doesn't know how many people to cook for.

4 What does Amanda enjoy most about her job?
- A ☐ meeting famous bands
- B ☐ working for young people
- C ☐ earning a lot of money

5 How does Amanda get to the place where she works?
- A ☐ by car   B ☐ by bus   C ☐ on foot

You can answer any questions you've missed when you hear the recording for a second time.

6 When she gets home in the evening, Amanda
- A ☐ writes about cooking.
- B ☐ cooks for her family.
- C ☐ listens to music.

Get ready for PET Listening Part 2

1 Listen to the instructions.
- How many people will you hear?
- Who are they?
- What are they talking about?

2 Read the questions quickly before you listen.
The questions are in the same order as the recording.
- Underline the most important word(s) in the question.
- Don't read the A, B, C options yet.

3 Listen to the recording. Can you hear the answers to the questions?

- Tick the box which best answers the question.

4 Listen again. Check that your answers are correct.

Remember:
- the questions are in the same order as the information on the recording.
- the answer will not always use exactly the same words as the recording.
- you may hear the words in all the options A, B, C on the recording.
- only one option, A, B or C answers the question.

4 Writing

Write a story which begins with this sentence:

Denis wanted to earn some money during the school holidays so he asked his uncle for a job.

Before you start to write, answer these questions.
- Where did Denis get a job?
- What kind of work did he do there?
- Who did he work with?
- How did he feel about the job?
- What happened unexpectedly one day?
- What did Denis do?

Write your story in about 100 words.

4 1 House and home

1 Which rooms do you have in your house?

dining room	kitchen	bedroom	garage
living room	bathroom	hallway	balcony
garden	stairs	storeroom	basement

Do you have any other rooms in your house?

2 In which room do you usually find these things? Divide them into the four groups. Some words can be used more than once.

dishwasher	wardrobe	chest of drawers	sink
coffee table	washbasin	armchair	dressing table
television	lamp	fridge	shower
cooker	towel rail	mirror	sofa

Living room	Kitchen	Bathroom	Bedroom

1 In the Speaking test, you talk about a photograph. If you don't know the word for something, you can say what it looks like, or what it is used for.

Example:

What's a coffee table?

It's a small, low table which you usually find in the living room. You can put things like cups of coffee, newspapers and magazines on it.

Talk about these things in the same way:

- a chest of drawers
- a towel rail
- a dishwasher
- a wardrobe
- a vase

2 Choose one of the photographs opposite and describe the room. Use the words in the box to help you talk about:

- the type of room it is
- what you can see in the room
- where the things are
- your opinion of the room
- who you think lives there

there's a/some
on top of
next to/beside
underneath/below
to the right of
to the left of
behind
in front of

24

A

B

3 **Listening** 🔊 1.12 **1** **Listen to a boy describing his room. Which room is his?**

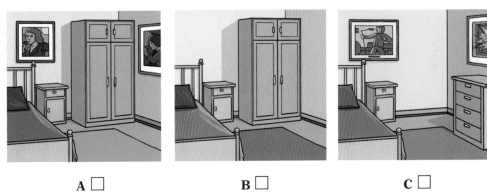

A ☐   B ☐   C ☐

2 **Describe your house. Talk about:**

- where it is
- what it looks like
- how many rooms it has
- your favourite room

4 **Writing**

Your English penfriend, who's called Chris, has never visited you and has asked you what your room is like.
Write a letter to Chris. In your letter, you should

- tell him how big your room is
- say what is in the room
- explain why you like it

Write 35–45 words.

5 **Listening** 🔊 1.13–16 **1** **Look at the three pictures. Where is the mobile phone in each picture?**

You hear each recording twice.
Read the questions carefully.
Only one picture answers the question.

A ☐

B ☐

C ☐

2 **What time does the film start?**

A ☐

B ☐

C ☐

3 **What does the woman decide to eat?**

A ☐

B ☐

C ☐

4 **Which piece of equipment does the woman need?**

A ☐

B ☐

C ☐

1 | **Vocabulary**

1 How often does your family get together for a celebration? Do you enjoy family parties? Why? Why not?

2 Find someone in the photo who:

is fair-haired	has curly hair	is in blue jeans	is smiling
is middle-aged	looks tired	is wearing glasses	is pointing

Now describe the photo. Begin like this:

'This is a picture of a family party. There are people of all ages here. Most of them are sitting down at a table, but two men …'

3 The words in the boxes describe people. In the first box, find seven pairs of words with *opposite* meanings.

attractive	careful	careless	cheerful	confident	miserable	foolish
hard-working	lazy	shy	strong	ugly	weak	wise

4 In this box, find seven pairs of words with *similar* meanings.

amusing	anxious	blond	boring	understanding	dull	fair
funny	honest	patient	slim	thin	truthful	worried

5 Which words describe you?

2 | **Writing**

You had arranged to meet your cousin at the station, but now you can't go. Write an e-mail to Robin, your English friend. In your e-mail, you should

- ask Robin to meet your cousin for you
- say why you can't go
- describe your cousin

Write 35–45 words.

3 Reading

1 Generally, how old are people when they first a) learn to read? b) go to university? Read the article about a boy who has done these things at a younger age than most people, and then answer the questions.

The most difficult thing for university student Shaun Rogers is opening his classroom door. Shaun can't do this without help because he's only six years old. He's the youngest person ever to study at Rochester University in New York. Shaun began reading at two, and by four was knowledgeable about a range of subjects from astronomy to zoology. By the age of five, he was regularly corresponding with university professors about his ideas. He has just completed his first book which will be published in a few months, shortly after his seventh birthday. 'I love learning,' says Shaun. 'My hero is the scientist Albert Einstein because he never combed his hair or wore socks.'

Psychologists have found it difficult to test Shaun's intelligence because it goes beyond what they usually measure. Shaun's mother first realized her son was different when he kept crying at playschool because he was bored with the children's games. She started teaching him at home after finding that local schools were not prepared for children who learnt at Shaun's speed. Now Shaun is studying geography at Rochester University and using the Internet to complete his high school studies.

However, some psychologists warn that too much study can prevent a child from developing normally. 'I don't care how brilliant the kid is, six-year-olds have to play with their friends,' says Dr Brian Wood. Mrs Rogers disagrees that her son's time is completely taken up by school work. 'He loves the violin and has many outdoor interests, such as camping, fishing and swimming, just like other boys his age.'

This question is asking you about the writer's purpose.

1 What is the writer trying to do in the text?
A advise parents about their children's education
B compare the development of normal and clever children
C encourage students to enter university at a young age
D interest people in the life of an unusual child

2 How old was Shaun when he wrote his first book?
A four
B five
C six
D seven

3 Why did Shaun's mother decide to educate him at home?
A because she couldn't find a suitable school for him
B because his school wouldn't let him use the Internet
C because his teachers were unkind and made him cry
D because he didn't get on with the other children

This question is asking you about Dr Wood's opinion.

4 What does Dr Wood think about Shaun?
A He isn't really any cleverer than other six-year-olds.
B He should spend more time having fun with other children.
C He will have to study harder to succeed at university.
D He can help his friends to do better at school.

You need to look at the whole text to answer this question.

5 Which of these is Mrs Rogers talking about Shaun?

A 'My son gets bored easily if he doesn't have other children to play games or go swimming with him.'

B 'My son loves his studies and fortunately there are many children of his own age in his class who share his interests.'

C 'What makes my son different from other children is that he started studying earlier and learns things much more quickly.'

D 'Like most young boys, my son often looks untidy and spends more time using the Internet than doing his homework.'

Get ready for PET Reading Part 4

1 The first question on this kind of reading text asks you about the writer's purpose. Has the writer of the text about Shaun succeeded in her/his purpose? In other words, has s/he interested you in Shaun's life?

2 In this kind of reading text, you have to understand people's *attitudes* and *opinions* as well as factual information. From this text, what do you understand about:

- Shaun's *attitude* to studying?
- Dr Wood's *opinion* about what six-year-old children need to do?
- Mrs Rogers' *opinion* about the amount of time her son spends studying?

3 In some of the questions in this kind of reading text, you have to look for the answer in more than one place. Look at question 5 and underline the two places in the text which give you the correct answer.

2 Match the writer's purposes with the sentences.

1 to recommend something	**A** Couples who decide to adopt a child should be prepared for the time when the child starts to ask difficult questions about the birth parents.
2 to compare two things	**B** Why do people using mobile phones in public places imagine everyone is interested in their conversations and speak in very loud voices?
3 to complain about something	**C** If, like me, you enjoy a film which keeps you sitting on the edge of your seat, then you shouldn't miss this one.
4 to explain something	**D** I felt close to my grandmother because she always met me from school and listened while I described the events of my day.
5 to warn against something	**E** Children with several brothers and sisters may feel differently from an only child when it comes to the school holidays.

4 Writing

Complete the second sentence so that it means the same as the first, using no more than three words.

1 That teacher is very patient with her students.

That is the teacher .... very patient with her students.

2 Shaun is too weak to open the classroom door.

Shaun isn't .... to open the classroom door.

3 In our class, only a few students have curly hair.

In our class, not .... curly hair.

4 My brother prefers funny films to serious ones.

My brother likes funny films .... serious ones.

5 'My favourite film star is Tom Cruise,' said my grandmother.

'Tom Cruise is the film star I like .... ,' said my grandmother.

1 Reading

1 Look at the notices, 1–10. Would you find them in a museum, a sports centre, a hotel, a giftshop or a post office?

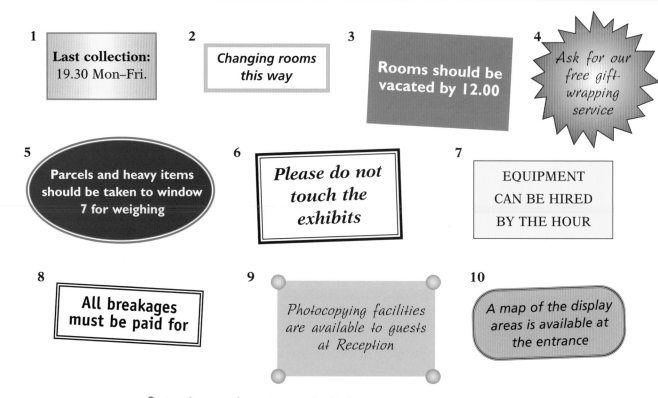

1
Last collection:
19.30 Mon–Fri.

2
*Changing rooms
this way*

3
Rooms should be
vacated by 12.00

4
*Ask for our
free gift-
wrapping
service*

5
Parcels and heavy items
should be taken to window
7 for weighing

6
*Please do not
touch the
exhibits*

7
EQUIPMENT
CAN BE HIRED
BY THE HOUR

8
All breakages
must be paid for

9
*Photocopying facilities
are available to guests
at Reception*

10
A map of the display
areas is available at
the entrance

2 Look at each notice again. Is it:

a) giving you information about what facilities are available?
b) telling you what you must or mustn't do?
c) giving you simple information, for example where or when?

3 Choose one place from the box below. What type of notices would you expect to see there? Write two examples of each type, a), b) and c).

school	department store	bank	airport

2 Listening 🔊 1.17–18

Get ready for PET Listening Part 3

1 Listen to the instructions.
• What are you going to listen to?
2 Read the notes quickly before you listen. The questions are in the same order as the recording.
• What type of information are you listening for in each question?
• Can you guess what the answers could be?

3 Listen to the recording. Can you hear the missing information?
• Write the missing information in the space.
• Write only one or two words.
4 Listen again. Check that your answers are correct.

Remember:
- the questions are in the same order as the information on the recording.
- you will hear the word(s) you have to write on the recording.
- you may hear other words that can fit the space – listen carefully.

- don't write more than one or two words (or sometimes a number).
- if the answer is a number, write the figure (for example 5), not the words.

Write only one or two words.
You hear the talk twice.

1 Look at the notes about Woburn Safari Park.
- You will hear a talk about a Safari Park.
- For each question, fill in the missing information in the numbered space.

WOBURN SAFARI PARK

It takes **(1)** .... to drive from London to Woburn Safari Park.

You travel around the park in **(2)** ....

In the park, you can see:
- lions and tigers
- giraffes
- elephants
- four different types of **(3)** ....

In the park, you are not allowed to have **(4)** ....

The park is open from Easter until the end of **(5)** .... each year.

After your tour of the park, you can visit:
- the children's playground
- the education centre
- the **(6)** ....

2 Look at the notes about Oxford Castle.
- You will hear part of a radio programme about the castle.
- For each question, fill in the missing information in the numbered space.

OXFORD CASTLE

How long it has been there:	**(1)** .... *years*
What it was used for in the past:	*it was a* **(2)** ....
What most of it is used for now:	*it is a* **(3)** ....
The main attractions for visitors:	*museum and* **(4)** ....
What you can do on the summer evenings:	**(5)** .... *in the open air*
Number to call for more information:	**(6)** ....

3 Reading

Look at the sentences about the Florida Keys area of the USA. Read the text and decide if each sentence is correct or incorrect.

1 The Florida Keys have a lot in common with other tourist attractions in Florida.
2 The main road through the islands is 200 miles long.
3 There are good opportunities to do underwater sports around the islands.
4 Visitors can choose from a wide range of places to stay in the islands.
5 The writer says that a good way to see the islands is to drive there from Miami.
6 Key West is a good place if you're looking for a relaxing life.
7 Mallory Dock is popular with local people as well as tourists.
8 It's a good idea to eat fish when you visit Mallory Dock.
9 You can see most of the Florida Keys in a short holiday.

THE FLORIDA KEYS

When you think of Florida, what comes to mind? Probably images of Disneyland, package holidays and burgers with extra relish. Well, the islands known as the Florida Keys couldn't be more unlike the mainland and that's one of the best kept secrets in the USA. Located between the Atlantic and the Gulf of Mexico, the Florida Keys are a line of islands that runs for 200 miles from the tip of Florida out into the ocean. The last island is just 90 miles away from the coast of Cuba. Along the way, there are islands, reefs, lakes, bays and beaches. From the largest island, Key Largo, to the tip of Key West, there are 43 bridges on the 126-mile Overseas Highway.

There really is something for everybody in the Florida Keys: excellent diving, a good range of theatres, museums, shops and restaurants; and every type of accommodation, from country camping places and family-owned guesthouses to the most luxurious hotels.

A good way to see the Keys is to take a flight from Miami to Key West, which takes half an hour. You can then hire a car and drive back to Miami, stopping at all the main attractions along the way. As you travel, you'll notice the green-and-white mile markers telling you how far you've come and how far you have to go.

Key West, the southernmost part of the USA, has a very laid-back attitude. For over a hundred years, it has been home to all sorts of people who want to avoid the stress of the mainland, especially artists and writers.

One part of the city you'll want to see is Mallory Dock, where the performances of street entertainers are enjoyed by locals and tourists alike. Once the sun has gone down, the open-air restaurants and bars come alive. Local seafood is superb and varied. If you're really brave you can even try fried alligator tail or, if you prefer, you can just dance all night.

To make the most of the food and culture on all the islands, you'd need to make your stay a long one. In fact, one of the most surprising things about Florida Keys is the number of visitors who decide to stay far longer than they had originally planned – some like it so much that they never go home again!

4 Speaking

1 **What are the main tourist attractions in your area**
• for young people?
• for older people?
• for foreign visitors?

2 **Talk about a historic building in your country and say what visitors can see and do there.**

Getting there

1 Vocabulary

1 Look at the words in the box. Divide them into four groups. Some of the words can be used more than once.

driver	pilot	attendant	land	catch	miss
get on	take off	check in	ticket	fare	station
take	platform	boarding pass	meter	timetable	gate

Taxi	Train	Bus/Coach	Plane

2 Complete the gaps in these sentences with words from the table.

1 If we don't hurry up, we'll .... the bus. It leaves the bus .... at ten o'clock.

2 It's cheaper for four people to .... a taxi rather than go on the underground, because the taxi .... comes to less than the price of four ....

3 After you .... your luggage, they give you a .... which you take along to the ...., where someone checks it before you .... the plane.

4 The train to Edinburgh leaves from .... number eight and you have to buy your .... in the office before you ....

5 In the ...., it said that the bus left at 10.00, and so we got there at 09.45 so that we would be sure to .... it.

2 Speaking

Look at the photograph and describe it. Make sure you answer these questions:

- Where was it taken? Who are the people? What is each of them doing? Why?
- What things can you see in the photograph?
- What are the people going to do next? Why?

What are the good and bad things about travelling by plane?

6 ① What a bargain!

1 Vocabulary

What's the difference between these pairs of words?
Example:
A jacket is shorter than a coat.
Check your answers in a dictionary.

coat/jacket   shirt/skirt
boot/shoe   socks/tights
tie/belt   wool/cotton
collar/sleeve   spots/stripes
pocket/bag   zip/buttons

2 Reading

Read these notices. Match them with the correct explanation, A, B, C or D.
There is one extra explanation.

1

> Changing rooms
> next to lift.
> Customers may take in no
> more than
> 4 pieces of clothing.

2

> Sorry!
> Lift to women's fashions
> out of order –
> Use escalator in TV
> department

3

> Today only!
> Prices on all
> electrical goods
> greatly reduced

A Because the lift isn't working, you'll have to go upstairs another way.

B You may not change any women's clothes you buy in today's sale.

C If you buy a television today, it will be much cheaper than usual.

D There's a limit to the number of clothes you may try on at one time.

3 Vocabulary

Read the sentences about money and find the missing words in the word square.
They are written from top to bottom, left to right, right to left and diagonally.

1 I don't _ _ _ _ a lot of money in my job, but I _ _ _ _ some every week for my holiday.

2 If you don't have cash, you can write a _ _ _ _ _ _ or pay by _ _ _ _ _ _ card.

3 If you don't put that _ _ _ _ in your wallet, and the _ _ _ _ in your pocket, you'll lose them before you can spend them!

C	S	L	S	A	V	E
H	C	H	E	Q	U	E
A	O	R	O	N	X	A
R	I	W	E	P	D	R
G	N	X	E	D	I	N
E	T	O	N	P	I	T
R	E	C	E	I	P	T

4 I got a _ _ _ _ _ _ _ when I bought these books for you, so you can see how much money you _ _ _ me.

5 Some people will borrow money from you, but they'll never _ _ _ _ it to you!

6 People like to _ _ _ _ in big department stores because everything they want is under one roof.

7 How much do you _ _ _ _ _ _ to repair shoes?

8 The service was very good here, so I'm going to leave the waitress a large _ _ _ .

4 **Writing**

1 **In PET Writing Part 3, you may write a letter to an English-speaking friend. Look at this example writing task.**

This is part of a letter you receive from an English penfriend.

> *I wanted to buy a T-shirt this morning but I had to go food shopping instead, which I hate. Do you like shopping? Are there any good stores near you?*

Now write a letter answering your penfriend's questions.
Write your letter in about 100 words.

2 **This is the letter one student wrote. Write the missing words.**

Dear Chris,
Thank you **(1)** .... your letter. I agree **(2)** .... you about food shopping. I hate **(3)** ...., too. The supermarket **(4)** .... always crowded and it's boring looking for rice **(5)** .... coffee!
  But I love shopping **(6)** .... clothes even though I **(7)** .... not got much money. My friends and I often **(8)** .... to the shopping centre in my town just to try **(9)** .... clothes. The shop assistants aren't very pleased when **(10)** .... don't buy anything!
  I also enjoy **(11)** .... to a music store in the shopping centre. I **(12)** .... hours there listening to **(13)** .... latest CDs. I always buy something, even if it's only **(14)** .... music magazine.
  Please write to **(15)** .... again soon.
Love,
Angela

- What is the topic of this letter? Is it what the 'English penfriend' wanted to hear about?
- What different kinds of shopping does Angela mention?
- What *reasons* does Angela give for disliking food shopping?
- What *examples* does Angela give of things she does when she's shopping?
- You start a letter with *'Dear ...'* followed by a 'hello' sentence. What 'hello' sentence does Angela use?
- You end a letter with a 'goodbye' sentence. What 'goodbye' sentence does Angela use?
- Look at these sentences. Find three 'hello' sentences and four 'goodbye' sentences.
  'Phone me or e-mail me and tell me what you think.'
  'I'm sorry I haven't written for a long time.'
  'I'm looking forward to your next letter.'
  'I was really pleased to hear your news.'
  'Give my best wishes to your family.'
  'It was great to hear from you again.'
  'See you soon.'
- At the end of a letter, you always sign your name. What does Angela write before her signature? Look at these phrases. Find two from an informal letter and one from a formal one.
  Yours sincerely,
  Best wishes,
  Yours,

Get ready for PET Writing Part 3

1 You have a choice in this part of the test. You have to write either a **letter** or a **story**. Read the instructions for both carefully and decide which one you can write best.

2 If you choose to write the **letter**, you will have to reply to something in a letter from an English penfriend. The penfriend's letter will tell you what the topic of your letter should be. Make sure you know what this topic is, eg 'shopping' or 'clothes'. Also make sure that you write about the topic given, and not about something else. Answer any questions your 'penfriend' asks.

3 In your **letter**, start with 'Dear ...,' and a 'hello' sentence. You should end with a 'goodbye' sentence, and sign your name.

4 If you choose to write the **story**, you will have either the title or the first sentence to guide you. Ask yourself some questions about your story before you start to write, for example: *Who ... ? Where ... ? When ... ? Why ... ? How did ... feel? What happened in the end?*

5 Your **letter** or **story** will look better if you write it in separate paragraphs, as Angela has done. Start each paragraph on a new line.

6 Try not to write fewer than 100 words, but don't write many more than 100.

7 When you've written your **letter** or **story**, check it carefully. Correct any grammar or spelling mistakes.

3 Write this letter.
This is part of a letter you receive from an English penfriend.

> I wore new shoes to a party last night and now my feet hurt. I hate wearing uncomfortable clothes! Tell me about the clothes you like and don't like wearing. What do you wear to parties?

Remember to organize your ideas in paragraphs. And check what you have written carefully.

Now write a letter telling your penfriend about the clothes you like.
Write your letter in about 100 words.

5 Listening 1.19 **Do you like shopping in street markets? Why? Why not?**
- Look at the advertisement for some street markets in London.
- Some information is missing.
- Listen to the man talking on the radio about the markets, and fill in the missing words.

East London Markets

Columbia Road
Over 50 stalls selling (1) .... at bargain prices.

Brick Lane
A market speciality is (2) ....

Petticoat Lane
Sells everything from clothes to toys.
Busiest day is (3) ....

Whitechapel
It's opposite (4) ....
Get your Asian vegetables and spices here.

Come and be part of the fun!

6 2 City life

1 Vocabulary

1 Look at these photographs. Choose one of the photographs and make a list of all the things you can see. Use the ideas to help you.

A  B

people   colours

objects   clothes

parts of the   buildings
vehicle

2 Answer these questions about your photograph.

1 What type of vehicle is it?
2 What type of street is it?
3 What are the people in the photo doing?
4 Why are they doing it?
5 How do you think they feel about it?

3 Now look at the other photograph and answer these questions.

1 What's the same or similar?
2 What's different?

2 Speaking

1 Which is better, living in a city or living in the country? Why?

2 Look at the adjectives in the box. Which would you use to describe
a) living in the city? b) living in the country?

calm	crowded	peaceful	clean	noisy
dirty	boring	relaxing	stressful	convenient
expensive	exciting	safe	lonely	interesting
fun	dangerous	polluted	inconvenient	

3 Make lists of the advantages of living in a) the city and b) the country.
Use the words in the box to help you.

shopping	night-life	fresh air	way of life	education
employment	transport	health	entertainment	

4 **Talk to another student. Decide who is Student A and who is Student B. Use your lists to have a discussion about life in the two places. Use some of the expressions below.**

Student A	**Student B**
Try to convince your partner that the city is the best place to live.	Try to convince your partner that the country is the best place to live.

One big
(dis)advantage of
the city/country is
that …

But we have
to remember that it is
easier to … in the
city/country.

Don't forget that
the city/country is much
more … than the
country/city.

Another thing
is that the city/country
is better for …

I'm afraid I
don't agree with
you because …

Yes, you're
right, but I still
think …

Get ready for PET Speaking Part 3

1 The examiner gives you a photograph of an everyday situation.
2 You talk on your own for about one minute.
• Tell the examiner everything you can see in the photograph.
• Talk to the examiner, not to your partner.
3 Remember:
• start immediately, and keep talking – don't stop and think.
• talk to the examiner, not your partner.
• talk about everything you can see.

• if you don't know the word for an object in the photograph, say what it looks like, or what it is used for.
• don't stop if you can't think of the word you need; talk about something else in the photograph.

5 **When you talk about the photograph, use these ideas to help you.**

1 Talk about the *place* in the photograph.
• Is it indoors or outdoors?
• Is it in a house or another building?
• What type of place is it?

2 Talk about the *people* in the photograph.
• How many people are there?
• What do they look like?
• What are they wearing?
• How do they feel?

3 Talk about *what's happening* in the photograph.
• What are the people doing?
• Why are they doing it?

6 Look at the photograph of some people in the countryside. Talk about it using the ideas in 5.

Talk to the examiner.

Tell the examiner everything you can see.

7 Look at the photograph of people in a city and talk about it. Remember:

* don't talk for more than one minute
* talk about everything you can see in the picture
* don't worry about words you don't know

Your partner will have a different photo.

8 Talk about a city you know. Say what you like about it and what you don't like about it.

1 Vocabulary

1 Look at the foods in the box. Divide them into the four groups.

carrots	beans	lamb	peas	onions	garlic
mushrooms	bananas	sausages	grapes	tomatoes	oranges
duck	pasta	beef	rice	chicken	leeks
olives	mayonnaise	tuna	butter	cheese	spinach
pepper	salt	steak	pizza	plums	burgers

Meat and fish	Vegetables	Fruit	Other

2 Add your favourite foods to the lists.

2 Speaking

1 Choose one of the photographs of people eating and talk about it. Remember to talk about everything you can see, including:
- each person – what they are doing, wearing and feeling
- the food and drink
- other things in the foreground
- things in the background

A

B

2 What is your favourite food? Talk about:

- breakfast
- dinner
- a snack
- a special meal
- a special treat

What do you drink with these foods?

Get ready for PET Speaking Part 4

1 In Part 4 of the PET Speaking test, you have a conversation with your partner. You only have a few minutes for the task.

2 The examiner tells you what to talk about, but does not ask you any questions.

3 The topic of Part 4 is the same as the one in the pictures in Part 3.

4 Remember:
- talk to your partner, not to the examiner
- ask your partner questions
- listen and respond to what your partner says
- don't talk for too long, and give your partner a chance to speak.

🎧 1.20 **3 Look at the photographs again and listen to the examiner's instructions for the Part 4 task. What is the topic of the conversation? Make a list of the things you can talk about and the questions you can ask your partner. Think about how to begin the conversation.**

Have the conversation with another student.

🎧 1.21 **4 Listen to two students beginning the task. As you listen, think about:**

- how they begin
- how long each person speaks for
- how they show interest in what each other says

5 Work with another student and do this Part 4 task. Don't talk for too long without involving your partner! Remember to ask questions and show interest. Use some of these phrases.

Ask your partner questions.

Show interest in what your partner says.

That's interesting because …

I like …, don't you?

I agree with you about that.

Really?

So do I!

Me too, and another thing is …

What about you?

Talk together about good restaurants you have been to and what you like to eat there.

3 Vocabulary

1 Look at the recipe and picture. Can you complete the gaps in the list of ingredients?

some different-sized ....
a small tin of ....
two spoonfuls of ....

a hard-boiled ....
some black ....
two spoonfuls of ....

What equipment do you think you need to make this recipe?

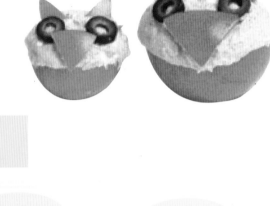

🔘 1.22 **Now listen and check your ideas.**

🔘 1.23 **2** How do you think you make this recipe? Use these verbs and the ingredients above to talk about it.

cut	mix	stir
pour	take out	

First you have to ...

Then you ...

Finally you ...

Now listen and check your ideas. Complete the table as you listen.

	Equipment	Verb	Ingredients
1			
2			
3			
4			
5			
6			
7			

4 Writing

Complete the second sentence so that it means the same as the first, using no more than three words.

1 In our house, the salad is usually prepared by my brother.
In our house, my brother .... the salad.

2 At breakfast, all the orange juice was finished.
At breakfast, someone .... orange juice.

3 My mother said: 'Don't burn the rice!'
My mother told .... burn the rice.

4 In the restaurant, Robbie asked for a burger and chips.
In the restaurant, Robbie said: 'Can .... a burger and chips, please?'

5 Martine suggested we ordered a pizza.
Martine said: 'Let's .... a pizza.'

7 2 Your own space

1 Speaking

Talk about how important each of these things is for you at home:
1 a room or space which is your own
2 a quiet place where you can relax or study
3 a place where you can make as much noise as you like
4 a place where you can invite your friends in comfort
5 your own special seat at the dining table
6 somewhere outside, for example a balcony or garden

2 Reading

1 Read this text about teenagers. Choose the correct word, A, B, C or D, for each space.

PERSONAL SPACE

More and more people live in large cities these days and this means that it is becoming more and more difficult to find space and time for ourselves. But for many people, personal privacy is very important. In many homes, a few minutes in the bathroom is all the privacy that is **(1)** ....

Teenagers especially need their own personal space at home where they can feel relaxed and private. But, of course, not all teenagers are **(2)** .... enough to have a room of their own. Where space is short, they often have to **(3)** .... a bedroom with a brother or sister. In that case, it's a good **(4)** .... for them to have a special area or corner of the room to **(5)** .... their own. It's especially important for young people to have somewhere to **(6)** .... their personal things. This may or may not be a tidy place and it is not a good idea for parents to try and tell teenagers how to **(7)** .... their space as this is **(8)** .... to lead to arguments. Parents can, however, **(9)** .... sure that there are enough storage spaces such as shelves, cupboards and boxes. This will **(10)** .... the teenager to keep their space tidy if they want to.

1	**A** confident	**B** available	**C** general	**D** average
2	**A** dizzy	**B** early	**C** lucky	**D** happy
3	**A** separate	**B** share	**C** divide	**D** join
4	**A** sense	**B** opinion	**C** idea	**D** thought
5	**A** mind	**B** call	**C** say	**D** tell
6	**A** belong	**B** save	**C** support	**D** keep
7	**A** organize	**B** repair	**C** operate	**D** review
8	**A** really	**B** quickly	**C** actually	**D** likely
9	**A** find	**B** make	**C** get	**D** put
10	**A** afford	**B** let	**C** allow	**D** set

2 Read the complete text again and answer these questions.

1 What is the writer trying to do in this text?

A complain about something

B blame someone for something

C give advice about something

D warn people about something

2 What does the writer believe?

A Teenagers can be selfish.

B Everybody needs some privacy.

C Parents can be unreasonable.

D Sharing is more important than privacy.

3 What does the writer think about tidiness?

A It is important for teenagers to be tidy.

B It is possible even when space is limited.

C It's a waste of time trying to be tidy.

D Parents should make their children be tidy.

3 Listening 🔊 1.24

Get ready for PET Listening Part 4

1 Part 4 of the PET Listening test is always a conversation between two people. They will be giving their opinions about something, and agreeing or disagreeing with each other.

2 Remember to read the instructions carefully to find out:
- who is talking
- where they are
- what they are talking about.
  This will help you to imagine the situation and understand what they say.

3 Remember to read the sentences on the question paper carefully to:
- make sure you know whose opinion the sentence is about
- check if the sentence matches the text or not.

4 You may not understand all the words in the text. Don't worry, you only have to answer six questions with YES or NO. If you're not sure, guess. You have a 50 per cent chance of being right!

1 Read the instructions for this Part 4 task.

- Look at the six sentences for this part.
- You will hear a conversation between a man, Bob, and a woman, Mary. They are talking about their teenage children.
- Decide if you think each sentence is correct or incorrect.
- If you think it is correct, put a tick (✓) in the box under **A** for **YES**. If you think it is not correct, put a tick (✓) in the box under **B** for **NO**.

Read the questions carefully.

2 Now listen and complete the task.

	A YES	B No
1 Mary's house is too small for Matthew to have his own room.	☐	☐
2 Matthew is a lot younger than his brother.	☐	☐
3 Bob wanted to spend more time alone as a teenager.	☐	☐
4 Matthew would like to have his own computer.	☐	☐
5 Mary feels that Matthew's brother has more need of a computer.	☐	☐
6 Matthew would like to watch the television more.	☐	☐

If you're not sure, then guess!

4 Speaking

What do you think?

1 How do you organize your personal space?
2 Do people respect your personal space?
3 Do you respect other people's space?
4 Do you think that tidiness is important?

5 Listening 1.25 **Now do this task.**

- Look at the six sentences.
- Alice and Harry are talking about their personal space.
- As you listen, decide if each sentence is correct or incorrect.
- If you think it is correct, put a tick (✓) in the box under **A** for **YES**. If you think it is not correct, put a tick (✓) in the box under **B** for **NO**.

		A YES	B NO
1	Alice regrets arguing with her mother.	☐	☐
2	Alice thinks her mother should put clothes away for her.	☐	☐
3	Alice tidies her room when she's expecting visitors.	☐	☐
4	Alice's wardrobe is too small for all her clothes.	☐	☐
5	Harry sometimes lets his brother wear his clothes.	☐	☐
6	Harry and his brother have to share a bedroom.	☐	☐

6 Speaking

Look at the two photographs. Talk about what you can see in each room.

A

B

1 Vocabulary — Use the words in the box to complete this text about the environment.
Write one word in each space.

| breathe | destroying | dusty | fuels | inhabitants | minerals |
| poverty | prevent | rescue | rubbish | spoil | urgent |

STOP DAMAGING THE EARTH!

We have spent the last one hundred years **(1)** .... our environment. In cities, factories and cars pollute the air we **(2)** .... , and everything we touch is **(3)** .... and dirty. We **(4)** .... the countryside by throwing away our **(5)** .... there, and ruin areas of natural beauty by digging up **(6)** .... , such as iron and gold, and **(7)** .... , such as coal and oil. While some people get rich, others suffer from **(8)** .... , hunger and disease. We must **(9)** .... this situation from getting worse. Finding a way to **(10)** .... our planet is an extremely **(11)** .... problem for all the **(12)** .... of the world.

2 Listening 🔊 1.26 **1 Last Saturday three people went out for the day. They each took a photograph.**

A   **B**   **C**

Listen to the three people talking about the weather on their day out and decide which photo each person took.

Speaker 1 ....   Speaker 2 ....   Speaker 3 ....

2 Listen to the three speakers again and write down all the weather words they use.

Good weather	Bad weather	Other weather words
fine	*storms*	*forecast*

3 Speaking — Talk about:
- weather that makes you feel cheerful/depressed
- clothes you wear in different kinds of weather
- activities you do in different kinds of weather
- the weather and holidays, celebrations and sports events

4 Reading · Read this text about gorillas. Choose the correct word, A, B, C or D, for each space.

Read the whole text first.

THE GORILLA

The gorilla is a shy creature and seldom violent. In **(1)** ...., it is quite different from the dangerous animal we sometimes see in films and comic books. It only stands up on two legs and beats its chest if it wants to **(2)** .... an enemy away.

Gorillas are the largest and **(3)** .... powerful of all the apes. Adult males reach an average height of 150–170 cm and **(4)** .... from 135 to 230 kg.

Females are smaller. **(5)** .... males and females are extremely strong and can tear down branches and pull up small trees. They **(6)** .... their days quietly in a leisurely **(7)** .... for food or resting in the warm sun.

Unfortunately, there are few of these animals **(8)** .... in the wild. This is mainly because people are cutting down the forests in **(9)** .... gorillas live. If we want to save the gorilla, we **(10)** .... take action now.

Try each word in the space before you choose the correct one.

1	**A** fact	**B** case	**C** place	**D** turn
2	**A** throw	**B** go	**C** frighten	**D** run
3	**A** very	**B** much	**C** more	**D** most
4	**A** count	**B** weigh	**C** add	**D** measure
5	**A** Every	**B** Either	**C** Each	**D** Both
6	**A** spend	**B** use	**C** do	**D** make
7	**A** inquiry	**B** search	**C** study	**D** examination
8	**A** remained	**B** stayed	**C** left	**D** continued
9	**A** what	**B** which	**C** that	**D** where
10	**A** must	**B** ought	**C** may	**D** have

Get ready for PET Reading Part 5

1 First read through the whole text to get a good idea of the general meaning.
2 Sometimes your knowledge of *vocabulary* is tested, for example in 4. Only one of these verbs (*count, weigh, add, measure*) makes sense in this sentence. Try each word in the space before you decide which one is correct.
3 Sometimes your knowledge of *grammar* is tested, for example in 3. Only one of these words (*very, much, more, most*) is correct here. Which one? Why are the other words incorrect?
4 Sometimes your knowledge of *vocabulary and grammar* is tested, for example in 8. You could use the verb *remain* in this sentence, but, to be correct, you should write *remaining*, and not *remained*.

5 Listening 🎧 1.27 **You will hear an interview on the radio with Henry Tweedy, who is talking about his special dog, Lady. Put a tick [✔] against the correct answer for each question.**

1 Henry needs his dog because he can't

A ☐ walk by himself.
B ☐ see anything.
C ☐ hear well.

2 Lady was chosen for training because

A ☐ she was friendly and intelligent.
B ☐ she already belonged to Henry.
C ☐ she was a young dog.

3 What does Henry say about Lady's training programme?

A ☐ It all happened in Henry's home.
B ☐ It is still going on.
C ☐ It took six months.

4 How does Lady communicate with Henry?

A ☐ by running around
B ☐ by touching him
C ☐ by making a noise

5 When Henry wants Lady to do something, he

A ☐ says certain words.
B ☐ uses a hand signal.
C ☐ gives her some food.

6 According to Henry, how does Lady feel about her work?

A ☐ She loves being active and useful.
B ☐ She would prefer to sleep more.
C ☐ She finds new things hard to learn.

6 Speaking

Discuss these questions.

1 Someone wants to give you an animal as a pet. Which one will you choose? Why?

| goldfish | kitten | duck | rabbit | mouse | monkey |

2 Which of these animals do you think helps humans most? Why?

| bee | chicken | cow | elephant | horse | dog |

3 Which of these animals would you be most afraid to meet? Why?

| spider | snake | shark | bat | tiger | bear |

7 Writing

This is part of a letter you receive from an English penfriend.

> I went horse-riding yesterday morning, and then I watched a brilliant TV programme about dolphins. I love all animals! How about you? Have you got a pet?

Now write a letter answering your penfriend's questions.
Write your letter in about 100 words.

1 Reading

1 **Would you like to tour a foreign country on a bicycle? Which countries do you think it would be good to visit in this way? Would tourists enjoy travelling through your country by bike?**

2 **Read the sentences about cycling in Sri Lanka. Then read the text and decide if each sentence is correct or incorrect.**

1 More people in Sri Lanka ride a mountain bike than any other kind of bike.
2 The writer says that you can go a satisfactory distance each day on a bike.
3 The writer says a bicycle is a restful way of travelling through Sri Lanka.
4 The canals provide water for rice growing in spaces in the jungle.
5 The writer admired the colours of the countryside.

On two wheels in a green land

It is often said that the best way to see a country is to use the method of transport which is traditional in that particular place. So people should see Argentina on horseback, Nepal on foot and the US by car. If this is true, then a bicycle is the perfect way to visit Sri Lanka. Although the 18-speed mountain bike I used is not an everyday sight, more traditional models are popular all over the country.

Sharing the same kind of transport as local people changes the way you see the place. You are travelling at a speed that somehow fits the scenery – not so slow that you only see a small area each day, and not so fast that the details of the countryside are missed. Better still, you can stop whenever you want to listen to the birds or a waterfall, talk to people, smell their cooking or take a photo. However, this doesn't mean cycling in Sri Lanka is relaxing. If you want to see the whole country, you have to leave the towns and villages and cycle through jungle, where the temperature is 37 degrees, cross streams, climb hills and go over paths which are made of mud, rock or sand.

The most pleasant paths in the jungle follow the irrigation canals. These carry water into the bright green rice fields which appear at regular intervals among the trees. During the afternoon, groups of children, farm workers and water buffalo all come to swim in the canals. Then, when you climb from the jungle up into the hilly area in the centre of the country, you see every hillside is covered with neat rows of tea bushes in another brilliant shade of green. In fact, the whole country is covered in more different and beautiful shades of green than I ever thought possible.

Now I'm wondering where to ride my bike next – perhaps alongside the canals of The Netherlands, or through the city streets of China ...

2 Vocabulary

Look at these groups of words. Which one is different? Why?
Example:

sea   ocean   bush   lake
bush *is different because it's not water.*

1 mountain   desert   cliff   hill
2 waterfall   country   continent   district
3 forest   wood   jungle   island
4 stream   canal   cave   river
5 bay   mud   sand   soil
6 path   road   track   wave
7 valley   coast   shore   beach
8 border   flood   frontier   edge

3 Speaking

Do you like adventure films? What difficulties and dangers do the heroes meet? Who do you want to win in this kind of film – the heroes or the villains? Imagine this situation.

• A famous director of adventure films wants your advice about the location of his next film. Here are some places where the action in the film may happen.

• Talk about the adventures the hero and heroine may have in each place and say which you think will be the most exciting.
• Which actors would you like to star in this film? Do you think it would be a popular film?

4 Writing

Remember the second sentence must mean the same as the first one.

Write one, two or three words in each gap.

1 **Here are some sentences about geography. Complete the second sentence so that it means the same as the first, using no more than three words.**

1 Britain is an island, so everywhere is near to the sea.
Britain is an island, so nowhere is .... the sea.
2 Never walk in the desert without taking water with you.
Take water with you if you're .... a walk in the desert.
3 Look at a map of the Indian Ocean if you want to find Sri Lanka.
You won't find Sri Lanka unless .... a map of the Indian Ocean.
4 I became a geography teacher five years ago.
I .... a geography teacher for five years.
5 The geography teacher asked if they wanted to watch a video.
The geography teacher said, 'Would .... watch a video?'

2 **Now look at these sentences about going to live in a different country. Complete the second sentence so that it means the same as the first, using no more than three words.**

Check what you have written carefully.

1 Yesterday, our passport photos were taken by a photographer.
Yesterday, a photographer .... our passport photos.
2 My suitcases are heavier than my brother's.
My brother's suitcases aren't .... mine.
3 At first, we'll have difficulty understanding the language.
At first, understanding the language will be .... us.
4 We have to find a flat before we can look for a school.
We can't look for a school until we .... a flat.
5 My brother and I have both promised to send e-mails to our friends.
I've promised to send e-mails to my friends and .... my brother.

Get ready for PET Writing Part 1

1 This part is a test of your grammar. Everything you write must be correct.
2 The second sentence *must* have the same meaning as the first sentence.
3 There are several different kinds of changes that you have to make. For example:
• find words with the opposite meaning. (1.1)
• change the order of the words. (1.2)
• change the tense of the verb. (1.4)

• change reported speech to direct speech. (1.5)
• make a passive sentence into an active one. (2.1)
• change the way you compare two things. (2.2)
4 Remember you may have to write one, two or three words in your answer. Never write more than three words. Contractions (eg *don't, I've*) count as two words.

5 Reading

Look at the messages. What does each one say? Choose A, B or C.

1

```
To:    Tyler
From:  Liza
.............................................
Can you record the
programme about the
world's oceans at 8.00 pm
for me? I forgot to set
the video before leaving
home. Thanks.
```

A Liza wants to make sure she doesn't miss a television programme.

B Liza wants Tyler to get a video for them to watch this evening.

C Liza wants Tyler to stay at home until a television programme finishes.

2

To Class 6B
Your projects on Antarctica are due in on Monday. Still need help? Then try the websites on the list on the noticeboard.
Mrs Barton

A Mrs Barton will see students who need help with their projects on Monday.

B Mrs Barton would like students to help her with a website about Antarctica.

C Mrs Barton says websites may help students finish their work on time.

1 Vocabulary

1 Rearrange these letters to make the names of sports.
Example:
TALLBOFO = football

1 FRIWGUSNNID   5 DOJU
2 BLATTNIESEN   6 COKYEH
3 FLOG   7 SEALLABB
4 STYGNIMCAS

2 Which of these sports do you like playing? What equipment do you need?
Which of these sports do you like watching? What skills must the players have?

2 Reading

What do you like to do in your school holidays?
- These people are all looking for a school holiday activity.
- Read the descriptions of eight school holiday activities on page 55.
- Decide which activity (letters **A–H**) would be most suitable for each person (numbers **1–5**).

1 Gwen is 18 and wants to take her younger brothers and sisters, aged between eight and 15, somewhere where they can get close to animals. She's just failed her driving test.

2 Matthew would like to take his daughter somewhere special on her sixth birthday, but he's only free in the afternoon. She loves hearing stories about animals but is frightened of real ones.

3 Lindsey has 11-year-old twin boys who hate sitting still. She wants to take them somewhere they can enjoy themselves safely all day while she goes to work.

4 Lewis is 15 and wants to do something exciting for the day with some friends from the school swimming team. They're keen to do something connected with either music or sport.

5 Jenny's going to look after her grandchildren, aged ten and seven, for the day. She can't afford to spend any money, but she'd like them to have some entertainment before she takes them home for lunch.

Holiday Fun
for Young People

A Pineapple Theatre Every day at 3 o'clock, young children (4–7 years) can watch 'Stardog'. The fun dog from space invents things to help earth people. At 5 o'clock, a group of 10–16-year-olds presents 'Football Fever', a play about young sports stars. All tickets £3.

B Queen's Arts Centre A day-long course for children (9–13 years) introduces the art of telling stories through music and poetry. Use your own history to make a musical piece. Younger children (4–8 years) may use rubbish to make musical instruments and then play them. No charge for entrance.

C Museum Gardens Circus skills workshop for children (7–11 years). Try juggling, rope walking and putting on clown make-up. Or watch Tiptop Theatre tell the story of a Native American boy and his horse. Both programmes 10–12 am. Entrance free.

D Sunshine Safari We have three floors of slides, swings, rope bridges and other adventure activities. Young adventurers can join a tiger hunt or swim with crocodiles. It all seems very real! Leave your children (3–14 years) in the care of our trained staff. £35 per day, lunch extra.

E Balloon flight See the countryside without having to drive! Our gas-filled balloon is tied to the ground and doesn't actually travel, but the views are fantastic. Price: £12 adult, £7.50 child. No under 5s, no children under 16 without an adult.

F Sea Life Centre Discover facts about life under the sea and watch many varieties of fish. The three-hour tour includes handling starfish, feeding sharks and swimming with dolphins. Adults £4.95, children £3.50.

G Making waves This adventurous programme for 12–18-year-olds gives you a chance to try your skills in a sailing boat, a canoe and a motor boat for just £12 a day. Full instruction is given. You must be a good swimmer and agree to follow all safety rules.

H Paradise Animal Park Drive your car through the park and get close to some of the world's most beautiful and dangerous animals. Younger visitors can have fun in the play area, while there is excitement for older children in the adventure playground with its 10-metre free-fall slide. Family ticket £25.

Get ready for PET Reading paper

1 You have 1 hour and 30 minutes for the Reading and Writing paper. Plan your time carefully.
2 There are five reading parts to the paper. Each part has a different kind of reading text with its own questions.
3 You can get 35 marks for the Reading paper, one mark for each question.
4 In the exam you get a question paper and an answer sheet (see p.88). You can make notes on the question paper but you must mark all your answers on the answer sheet.
5 You must use pencil on the answer sheet. Take a pencil, pencil sharpener and rubber to the exam.
6 Read the texts carefully, but don't worry if there are words you don't understand. You probably don't need to know them to answer the questions.
7 Mark one letter for each question. To make a change, rub it out carefully and mark the new answer clearly.
8 If there is a question you can't answer, leave it and go back to it later.
9 Near the end of the test time, check your answers and make sure you have marked an answer for everything. If you don't know something, guess – you may be right!
10 There is more information about this paper in the **Get ready** boxes in this book. Make sure you read them again before the exam.

3 Vocabulary

1 These people are all planning to do their favourite free-time activity. What does each person need? Choose the words from the box.

I'm going to make a skirt to wear to the party tomorrow.

I'm going to decorate my bedroom and put up some shelves.

I'm going to answer this letter from my penfriend.

I'm going to do some work in the garden.

I'm going to have a game of tennis.

 **1**

 **2**

 **3**

 **4**

 **5**

balls	brush	dictionary	envelope	flower pot	net
hammer	material	nails	needle	notepaper	
racket	paint	scissors	pins	watering can	
seeds	spade	sports bag	stamp	refreshing drink	

2 What's your favourite free-time activity? What do you need to do it?

4 Speaking

A friend of yours has just moved to a different town and wants to take up a hobby that will help him/her make new friends. Here are some pictures of some hobbies s/he could do.

- Talk about how interesting the different hobbies are, and decide which will be best for making friends.

1 Writing

1 Do you think you have a healthy lifestyle? What makes your lifestyle healthy or unhealthy?

2 You and your English friend, Alex, have decided to have a more healthy lifestyle.
Write an e-mail to send to Alex. In your e-mail, you should

- tell Alex about your new sleeping habits
- say what type of food you plan to eat in future
- suggest some exercise or sport you can do together

Write 35–45 words.

2 Vocabulary

Read the sentences about health and sickness and find the missing words in the word square. They are written from top to bottom, left to right, right to left and diagonally.

1 This is an _ _ _ _ _ _ _ _ _ ! Some people have been hurt in a road _ _ _ _ _ _ _ _ , and they need an _ _ _ _ _ _ _ _ _ to take them to hospital.
2 I have bad _ _ _ _ _ _ _ so the doctor sent me to the ear _ _ _ _ _ _ at the hospital. Now I have to take a _ _ _ _ three times a day to make the _ _ _ _ go away.
3 A _ _ _ _ person can't hear without the help of a hearing aid.
4 A doctor and a _ _ _ _ _ both work in a hospital. A _ _ _ _ _ _ _ is a sick person they look after.
5 Even if we had a _ _ _ _ to cure every disease, would everyone be _ _ _ and healthy?
6 Doctor, I feel really _ _ _ . I've got a cold, a _ _ _ _ throat, and a high temperature. And just listen to my horrible _ _ _ _ _ ! I think I've got _ _ _ .
7 When I cut myself with a bread knife, the _ _ _ _ _ was quite deep. There was a lot of blood so my face went _ _ _ _ , I felt _ _ _ _ _ and thought I was going to fall over, but fortunately I didn't _ _ _ _ _.

A	M	B	U	L	A	N	C	E
C	L	I	N	I	C	U	P	M
C	S	E	H	C	A	R	A	E
I	O	Q	P	J	P	S	T	R
D	R	U	G	I	A	E	I	G
E	E	K	G	F	L	U	E	E
N	I	A	P	H	E	L	N	N
T	T	I	F	A	I	N	T	C
W	O	U	N	D	I	Z	Z	Y

3 Reading

Read the text and questions. For each question, decide which is the correct answer, A, B, C or D.

" I'm sure I'm not the only person my age (15) who hates going to the dentist. Channel 4's late-night documentary *Open wide* last Tuesday was excellent for people like me. However, none of my school friends watched it. They missed this opportunity to see something interesting and educational because the programme didn't appear in the *TV Guide*. This was a pity, as it was the type of programme that makes both young people and their parents think about things they don't normally consider. Why can't television companies let us know about such important documentaries in advance?

This programme was important because it showed how methods for helping people with toothache have developed over the centuries. If you think visiting the dentist today is an uncomfortable experience, just be grateful you didn't live 200 years ago! Then, the programme told us, the only cure for toothache was removing the tooth. There weren't any dentists, so the person who cut your hair also pulled out your bad teeth, and there was nothing to stop you feeling the pain.

The programme has also completely changed my attitude to looking after my teeth. My parents were always saying to me things like, 'Don't eat too many sweets,' and, 'Brush your teeth after meals,' but I never paid much attention. Now I've seen what damage sugar can do, especially if I don't use a toothbrush regularly, I'm going to change my habits. Many people would benefit from a repeat of this programme. "

Sophie Ashley, Oxford

1 Why has Sophie written this letter?
A to complain about the time a television programme was shown
B to ask for more television programmes designed for school children
C to advise people to watch a particular television programme
D to persuade a television company to show a programme again

2 Why didn't Sophie's school friends see *Open wide*?
A They didn't know it was on.
B They don't enjoy that type of programme.
C Their parents wouldn't let them.
D It wasn't shown on a channel they can receive.

3 What did *Open wide* say about toothache?
A In the past, nobody could make it stop.
B Dentists used to help people who had it.
C Hairdressers have it more than other people.
D Ways of curing it have changed.

4 What does Sophie think about her parents now?
A They don't know as much as her about teeth.
B Their advice is worth listening to.
C They eat things which are bad for them.
D They don't clean their teeth often enough.

5 Which of these gives information about the programme Sophie watched?

A A play about a 19th-century dentist and how he brought comfort to his patients.

B The series about health care for teenagers. This week, good eating habits.

C This history of the dentist's profession shows what happens when we eat.

D We suggest how to prepare young children for that first visit to the dentist.

4 | **Writing**

Complete the second sentence so that it means the same as the first, using no more than three words.

1 Last night, I took an aspirin to stop my head aching.
Last night, I took an aspirin because .... aching.

2 My brother goes jogging because he must keep fit for his job.
My brother goes jogging to .... for his job.

3 If you don't give up coffee, you'll never sleep well.
You'll never sleep well unless .... coffee.

4 People with flu should stay in bed for a few days.
Stay in bed for a few days if you .... flu.

5 Smoking isn't allowed in hospitals.
You .... in hospitals.

5 | **Writing**

Write one of the following questions.

1 **This is part of a letter you receive from an English penfriend.**

I've got flu. I feel terrible and I'm bored because I have to stay in bed. What can I do to make myself feel more cheerful? Tell me about the last time you were ill.

Now write a letter answering your penfriend's questions.
Write your letter in about 100 words.

2 **Your English teacher has asked you to write a story.**
This is the title for your story:
The keep fit class

Write your story in about 100 words.

Get ready for PET Writing paper

1 You have 1 hour and 30 minutes for the Reading and Writing paper. The writing comes at the end of the paper, so plan your time carefully.

2 There are three writing parts to the paper: completing sentences, writing a short message and writing a letter or story.

3 You can get 25 marks for the Writing paper: 5 marks for Part 1, 5 marks for Part 2 and 15 marks for Part 3.

4 In the exam, you get a question paper and an answer sheet (see p.88–89). You can make notes on the question paper but you must write your answers on the answer sheet.

5 Write clearly. You don't want to lose marks because the examiner can't read your writing!

6 When you do Part 1, make sure that you don't write more than three words for any answer.

7 When you do Part 2, remember to write something about each point in the instructions.

8 When you do Part 3, try to make your letter or story clear and interesting.

9 Near the end of the test time, check your answers.

10 There is more information about this paper in the **Get ready** boxes in this book. Make sure you read them again before the exam.

Entertainment

1 Speaking

1 How often do you do these things?

watch television	sometimes
go to the cinema	quite often
surf the Internet	not very often
go to a concert	occasionally
go to the theatre	very often
go clubbing	never

2 Match the things in this box with the different types of entertainment.

curtain	encore	website	commercial
interval	soap opera	programme	backing group
ticket	channel	soloist	chat room

3 Say what you like and dislike about each type of entertainment.

2 Vocabulary

1 Complete the text with words from the box. Use each word only once.

part	clap	reviews	rehearsal	screen	camera
performance	series	director	stage	studio	lines

An actor speaks ••••••••••••••••••••••••••••••••••••

As an actor, I much prefer working in the theatre to working on a film or a television **(1)** .... When I get a **(2)** .... in a play, I spend a long time learning my **(3)** .... and then there is a long period of **(4)** .... with the other actors before the first night. The good thing about a play, however, is that you are standing up on the **(5)** .... with a real live audience just a few metres away from you. At the end of the play, if they have enjoyed it, the people all **(6)** .... and you really feel good. It's interesting to read the **(7)** .... in the newspaper, but it's the people who are there who really matter.

Working in film or television, however, you spend too much time waiting in the **(8)** .... while the **(9)** .... crew make all the technical arrangements. You sometimes have to do the same bit over and over again until the **(10)** .... is satisfied with your **(11)** .... Then it is months or even years before the film or programme appears on the **(12)** .... By then, you've forgotten all about it and you're in the middle of doing the next thing, anyway.

2 Choose the best answer, A, B, C or D.

1 Why does the actor prefer working in the theatre?

A You have lots of time to practise.

B It's the same every night.

C There is a live audience.

D He always gets good reviews.

2 What does the actor dislike about working on films?

A It can be boring.

B You can get lonely.

C It is easy to forget your lines.

D You have to do two things at once.

3 **Fill in the missing word in these sentences.**

1 A .... is someone who writes in a magazine or newspaper.

2 A guitarist is someone who .... a guitar, often in a group.

4 **Make similar sentences to explain what these people do.**

drummer	director	photographer	TV presenter
disc jockey	comedian	pianist	film critic
interviewer	dancer	singer	violinist

3 Listening 1.28–30

1 **Listen to two friends discussing what to do this evening. Where do they decide to go?**

A ☐

B ☐

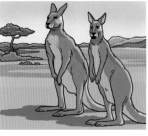
C ☐

2 **Listen to two friends talking about films. Which type of film do they decide to go and see?**

A ☐

B ☐

C ☐

3 **Listen to two friends discussing a film they have each seen. What did they like most about the film?**

A the plot

B the actors

C the camerawork

4 Speaking

Talk about a film, play or TV programme you have seen recently. Say what was good and bad about it. Remember to include information about the plot, camerawork and actors.

5 Listening 🔊 1.31

Get ready for PET Listening paper

1 You have about 30 minutes for the Listening paper.
2 There are four parts to the paper: Part 1 has seven short texts, and Parts 2, 3 and 4 have one long text each.
3 You can get 25 marks for the Listening paper, one for each question.
4 There are pauses between the listening texts. Make sure you use this time to read the questions for the next part, so you are ready to answer.
5 You hear each listening text twice. Answer the questions during the first listening. Check your answers when you hear the text for the second time.
6 In the exam you get a question paper and an answer sheet (see p.89). As you listen, write your answers on the question paper. At the end of the test, you have extra time to copy your answers on to the answer sheet.

7 You must use pencil on the answer sheet. Take a pencil, pencil sharpener and rubber to the exam.
8 Copy your answers carefully on to the answer sheet. Mark only one letter for each question. If you make a mistake, rub it out carefully and mark the new answer clearly.
9 Listen carefully, but don't worry if there are words you don't understand. You probably don't need to know them to answer the questions.
10 If there is a question you can't answer, just leave it and move on to the next one. You will probably hear the answer the second time you listen.
11 If you don't know the answer after the two listenings, guess – you may be right!
12 There is more information about this paper in the **Get ready** boxes in this book. Make sure you read them again before the exam.

Now try this listening task. Listen twice, as in the exam.
- Look at the notes about radio programmes.
- Some information is missing.
- You will hear an announcement about the programmes.
- For each question, fill in the missing information.

THIS MORNING'S RADIO

08.00	News
(1).......	*Arts Review* programme
	– information about theatre, concerts and films
	– special guest: Kevin Jones, (2) .... in a pop band.
08.45	(3) .... with Graham Smith.
08.50	New series: Polly Brown talks to people about (4) ....
09.30	(5) .... with James Grant.
10.15	Radio play called (6) '............'

---

6 Writing

Your English teacher has asked you to write a story.
Your story must begin with this sentence:

When the taxi came, Sandra was ready in her best dress and shoes.

Write your story in about 100 words.

The age of communication

1 Speaking

1 **Look at these ways of keeping in touch with people.**

| letters | mobile phone | e-mail | fax | pager |

Talk about:
- how often you use each one
- what you use each one for
- the good and bad things about each one

2 **Look at these two photographs. They both show people keeping in touch with their friends. Choose one of the photographs and talk about it. Remember to talk about all the things you can see, what the people are doing, and how you think they are feeling.**

A

B

Get ready for PET Speaking paper

1 You have 10–12 minutes for the Speaking paper.

2 You take the test with another student who is your partner. There are two examiners: one tells you what to do and the other one listens. Remember to speak clearly so both examiners can hear you.

3 There are four parts to the paper: talking about yourself, a situation, a photograph, and discussing a wider theme.

4 You can get 25 marks for the Speaking paper. You get marks for how well you communicate with your partner and for your pronunciation. There are also some marks for grammar and vocabulary.

5 Listen carefully to the examiner's instructions. If you are not sure what to do, ask the examiner to repeat them.

6 In Parts 2 and 4, talk to your partner – not to the examiner.

7 In Parts 2 and 3 the pictures are there to help you. Talk about what you can see and don't stop after you have talked about one thing. If you can't remember the word for something, don't worry. You can describe the thing or talk about something else.

8 Try to make the test easier for your partner and the examiner by being relaxed and friendly. In Parts 2 and 4, remember to ask your partner questions, show an interest in what they say, and give them a chance to speak.

9 There is more information about this paper in the **Get ready** boxes in this book. Make sure you read them again before the exam.

3 Practise this Part 2 task with a friend. Remember to talk about *all* the pictures, and don't decide too soon!

The examiner says:

I'm going to describe a situation to you. A friend is going away to study in another town. She will be living on her own in a student flat. She has some money to spend on one piece of electrical equipment, but she doesn't know what to buy. Talk together about the different things she can buy, and then say which will be best.

4 Remember, you will be asked to spell your name in Part 1 of the test. Practise spelling these words out loud in English:

*   your first name
*   your family name

2 Reading   **Read the text below and choose the correct word, A, B, C or D, for each space.**

THE RECIPE FOR GOOD COMMUNICATION

How many people do you communicate with in a day? Probably a lot more **(1)** .... you did ten years ago. With a few pieces of equipment, we can 'talk' to people in more and more ways, not **(2)** .... face-to-face and on the phone, but also via the Internet. It is very important, therefore, **(3)** .... everyone to try and improve their communication skills. Despite all the technological advances of **(4)** .... years, the art of good conversation is still at the heart of successful communication. **(5)** .... it's a good idea to remember the four golden rules of good communication. Firstly, be as clear as you can. Misunderstandings arise if we don't say exactly **(6)** .... we mean. Secondly, we have to work **(7)** .... at listening. Pay attention to what the other person is saying. Thirdly, ask **(8)** .... people what they think, don't only tell them what you think. And finally show respect for people, give them time to say what they want, and **(9)** .... interest in what they say.
If you **(10)** .... these rules, you will be a good communicator.

1	**A** like	**B** than	**C** as	**D** that
2	**A** yet	**B** even	**C** just	**D** still
3	**A** for	**B** if	**C** by	**D** from
4	**A** close	**B** last	**C** late	**D** recent
5	**A** There	**B** So	**C** Such	**D** Or
6	**A** when	**B** what	**C** which	**D** whom
7	**A** hard	**B** much	**C** great	**D** very
8	**A** every	**B** other	**C** each	**D** another
9	**A** get	**B** put	**C** be	**D** show
10	**A** act	**B** move	**C** follow	**D** go

3 Writing   **Complete the second sentence so that it means the same as the first, using no more than three words.**

1   My parents prefer using the telephone to using e-mail.
    My parents think using the telephone is better .... e-mail.
2   My neighbour is confused by modern technology.
    Modern technology .... my neighbour.
3   Whose is this mobile phone?
    Who does this mobile phone .... to?
4   When I look at a screen for too long, I find it tiring.
    I get .... when I look at a screen for too long.
5   Why don't you send Anne a text message?
    If I were you, ... send Anne a text message.

PAPER 1   Reading and Writing Test   1 hour 30 minutes

READING

PART 1

Questions 1–5

Look at the text in each question.
What does it say?
Mark the correct letter **A**, **B** or **C** on your answer sheet.

Example:

0

> **These animals are
> dangerous.
> Do not cross the
> safety fence.**

- **A** Don't get any nearer to these animals because they may hurt you.
- **B** Don't let these animals get out from behind this fence.
- **C** It's dangerous to bring animals into this area.

Answer:

Part 1		
0 A B C		
▬ ☐ ☐		

1

> **Passengers' hand luggage
> must fit safely in the
> overhead lockers –
> if not, check it in**

- **A** Passengers may take hand luggage unless it's too big for the overhead lockers.
- **B** Passengers are not allowed to put any hand luggage in the overhead lockers.
- **C** Passengers must close the overhead lockers after fitting in their hand luggage.

2

To: Mariella
From: Bruno

My washing machine's
broken down again. Is it
OK if I bring my washing
round this evening? We
can order pizza and have
a chat.

- **A** Bruno intends to mend his washing machine before ordering pizza for himself and Mariella.
- **B** Bruno wants to help Mariella do her washing and make her pizza for dinner.
- **C** Bruno is planning a pleasant evening at Mariella's while he does his washing there.

3

> **SAME-DAY DELIVERY**
>
> on all flowers ordered
> before 2 p.m.

- **A** Order from us today and we will deliver your flowers by 2 p.m.
- **B** If you place an order by 2 p.m., we can deliver your flowers today.
- **C** Flowers are delivered at about 2 p.m. on the day after the order is made.

4

Tom
I'll be late this evening so
can you record the football
match? Then we can watch it
together when I get home.
Dad

- **A** Dad would like to go to a football match with Tom.
- **B** Dad doesn't want Tom to watch the football match without him.
- **C** Dad hopes to get home before the football match begins.

5

> *Please consider your
> neighbours and keep your
> music down after 11 p.m.*

- **A** Think of your neighbours and switch your music off at 11 p.m.
- **B** Please play your music so your neighbours can hear it until 11 p.m.
- **C** Your neighbours may want to sleep so don't play loud music later than 11 p.m.

PART 2

Questions 6–10

The people below all want to study English in Britain.
On the opposite page, there are descriptions of eight language schools.
Decide which language school would be the most suitable for the following people.
For questions **6–10**, mark the correct letter (**A–H**) on your answer sheet.

6

Akiko, from Japan, is 19 and hoping to go to a British university to study fashion. First she'll spend a year at a language school in London improving her English and living with English people.

7

Luiz Carlos is studying medicine in Brazil. He'd like to spend next February in any British city studying the kind of English that will help him in his future career. He'll find his own accommodation.

8

Hanna is an English teacher from Poland. She's planning to spend August at a school somewhere outside London where she can do a teacher training course. She'd like accommodation to be provided.

9

Yusuf, from the Ivory Coast, speaks almost no English and would like to study hard for six months to get a recognized qualification. He'll be happiest living outside London in a hostel with other students.

10

Elena, from Spain, wants to bring her two daughters aged 9 and 11 to a school at the seaside for two weeks in July. It's important they enjoy themselves while improving their English.

ENGLISH SCHOOLS IN THE UNITED KINGDOM

A English Now

This school has just opened in London with the aim of providing English classes (30 hours per week) from July to September for students from other countries going to study at British universities. Students stay with English families or in a student hostel.

B Phillips Academy

This school in the Scottish capital of Edinburgh has courses for students who need to use English in their work. There are courses in English for business, for tourism, and for health service workers. Courses are available throughout the year. Rooms with local families can be arranged.

C Language Centre

This school is in a wonderful location on the coast four hours from London. There are classes for all ages (starting at age 8) between March and October (minimum stay one week). Teachers aim to make lessons fun and there are visits to places of interest in the afternoons. Accommodation is in guest houses.

D Walton College

This seaside school, 300 kilometres from London, offers course of either 2 or 4 weeks between June and September. Courses are for adults, for children aged 12 to 16, and for people wanting to improve their English teaching skills. There are trips organized every afternoon. Students live in single and shared rooms in the college.

E Drake English School

This school has branches in nine cities in the United Kingdom, but not London. Each branch offers classes (25 hours per week) for students at intermediate and advanced levels and provides special preparation for a number of recognized English exams. Students must register for at least one month. Accommodation is provided with English families.

F MPS Language Services

Situated in the centre of London, this language school offers year round courses (20 hours per week) at all levels for students aged 18 or over. Study advisers help with British university applications and work experience placements. Accommodation can be arranged with English families or in student hostels near the school.

G Turner House

This school in the northern city of Leeds offers a range of specialist advanced English courses, including English for business, for the hotel industry, and for doctors. There are also teacher training courses for experienced English teachers. Courses take place from April to November. Accommodation cannot be booked for students by the school.

H Dixon Hall

This school is situated in beautiful countryside three hours from London. There are classes (25 or 30 hours per week) at all levels from beginner to advanced. As students are encouraged to take one of a range of international exams, they usually stay from 3 to 12 months. Students stay in international student hostels.

PRACTICE TEST 1 – READING

PART 3

Questions 11–20

Look at the sentences below about a holiday on a cruise ship.
Read the text on the opposite page to decide if each sentence is correct or incorrect.
If it is correct, mark **A** on your answer sheet.
If it is not correct, mark **B** on your answer sheet.

11   A holiday on a cruise ship is suitable for children.

12   August is the most popular time to go on a cruise.

13   Staff on board will help parents by looking after their children while they play.

14   Passengers are encouraged to wear smart clothes at dinner time.

15   The ship's crew work as calmly behind closed doors as they do in public.

16   The ship's captain prefers to use technology as much as possible when sailing the ship.

17   If you book your cruise some time in advance, you may pay less.

18   It is difficult to find out how large your tips should be.

19   You are recommended to use e-mail rather than the satellite phone to contact people on land.

20   Being seasick on board is a common problem.

Holiday at Sea

My wife and I had never considered a cruise holiday because we have four children under fourteen and we didn't think a ship could offer the kind of facilities that kids enjoy. But we found we were wrong when we took a 9-day trip on the Caribbean Princess, a ship which can carry over three thousand passengers. We travelled last August, and so the ship was nearly full although more people go in July. We boarded the boat in Florida and our destinations were the Bahamas, Jamaica, the Cayman Islands and Mexico, which are all beautiful places to visit.

On board, my children had special clubs to go to so they always had plenty to do with people of their own age, while my wife and I could relax knowing professionals were keeping an eye on them. The on-board facilities were fantastic, including great shops, a jogging track, basketball courts and a range of excellent restaurants. Many people dress up for dinner and my family loved doing that but nobody makes you feel uncomfortable if you just wear ordinary clothes. After dinner, there's a choice of first class entertainment.

I wanted to find out what was involved in running such a big ship so I went through doors I wasn't really supposed to open! Out front, everything is calm and efficient, but behind the scenes there are people running around and working like mad. I was lucky enough to go on the bridge from where the captain sails the ship. There's an enormous amount of modern technology there but, being a real seaman, he likes to do as much as he can by hand.

I would definitely recommend a cruise holiday to anyone but make sure you search for the best possible price. You may get as much as a 45 per cent discount for an early booking. On the other hand, no cruise ship will leave half-empty so you might be able to get a last-minute, cheap ticket. Tipping is expected so you can save some money for that. Don't worry about what amount to give because you'll be told.

You'll want to keep in touch with people back home while you are away but remember that most mobile phones don't work at sea. You can make a satellite phone call from a cruise ship but that can cost as much as £9 per minute, so it's better to use the on-board e-mail service or wait until the next port to use a landline phone.

Unless you run into unusually bad weather, it is unlikely you'll be seasick. Most cruise ships are very large and specially designed so that they don't roll around in high seas.

PART 4

Questions 21–25

Read the text and questions below.
For each question, mark the correct letter **A**, **B**, **C** or **D** on your answer sheet.

Bertrand Piccard and his co-pilot Brian Jones were the first people to fly around the Earth in a balloon non-stop in 1999.

I learnt to fly in a balloon in a race across the Atlantic Ocean in 1992 and became fascinated by the sport. In the same way that a mountain climber dreams of climbing the world's highest mountain, I dreamed about flying non-stop around the world.

I spent six years planning the flight and failed twice before we managed to succeed. Our route took us over China, but we could only get permission to travel over the south. This meant going first to North Africa to catch the right winds. That added 10,000 kilometres, and another week, to our journey. But because of this, our flight broke all the records for distance and time spent in the air.

My main memory of the trip is that we lived in the air for 20 days and that the rising sun was the most amazing thing we saw. We had to go out of the balloon's capsule, in which we were transported, three times while in the air to repair the fuel system. We didn't have any safety equipment but when you are in a situation like that, you just do what you have to do without thinking about feeling afraid.

Landing was a fantastic moment. I remember that when I got out of the capsule, I looked at my footprint in the sand. I remembered the astronaut Neil Armstrong who was so happy to put his footprint on the moon, so far away from Earth. At that moment, I was so happy to have my foot back on Earth!

---

21 What is Bertrand Piccard's main reason for writing this text?

- **A** to compare the sport of ballooning with mountain climbing
- **B** to recommend ballooning as a means of transport
- **C** to describe the lessons that failure has taught him
- **D** to report on succeeding at something he'd dreamt of for years

22 Why did the balloon fly over south China?

- **A** The wind took it in the wrong direction.
- **B** The pilots weren't allowed to cross any other part.
- **C** The pilots were running out of time.
- **D** That route made the journey shorter.

23 Why did the pilots get out of the capsule during the flight?

- **A** to practise what to do in an emergency
- **B** to check the safety equipment was working
- **C** to mend something which had a fault
- **D** to test their courage in a dangerous situation

24 How does Piccard say he felt when he landed?

- **A** pleased to see a sign that he'd returned to Earth
- **B** proud to be told he was like Neil Armstrong
- **C** not able to stand or walk properly
- **D** like an astronaut returning from the moon

25 What was the newspaper headline after the balloon landed?

- **A** Balloon pilot flies alone around the world
- **B** Non-stop from North Africa to China
- **C** Magnificent record flight for Piccard and Jones
- **D** New record – 10,000 km in a week

PART 5

Questions 26–35

Read the text below and choose the correct word for each space.
For each question, mark the correct letter **A, B, C** or **D** on your answer sheet.

Example answer:

0	**A** near	**B** close	**C** about	**D** across

Part 5

| 0 | A ■ | B ☐ | C ☐ | D ☐ |

ISLAND FESTIVAL

Cheung Chau is a small island **(0)**...... Hong Kong in the South China Sea that has a colourful festival each spring. The main **(26)**...... of the festival is a procession through the streets in **(27)**...... children dressed in beautiful costumes are carried high in the air on long bamboo sticks. The children **(28)**...... to fly and the man who teaches them to do this is retired schoolteacher Yeung Yuk Lun. **(29)**...... child on the island hopes to be chosen to **(30)**...... part. 'Obviously, the children **(31)**...... to be small and light,' says Yeung Yuk Lun. 'This **(32)**...... they are usually between four and seven years old. They are extremely brave **(33)**...... it's quite frightening to be up in the air above a noisy crowd.' Towers of cakes are carried beside the children and offered to the ancient god Pak Tai, who, **(34)**...... to an old story, once **(35)**...... the island from great danger.

26	**A** demonstration	**B** attraction	**C** invitation	**D** composition
27	**A** it	**B** this	**C** which	**D** what
28	**A** appear	**B** look	**C** play	**D** show
29	**A** Every	**B** All	**C** Most	**D** Many
30	**A** make	**B** do	**C** get	**D** take
31	**A** must	**B** should	**C** will	**D** have
32	**A** supposes	**B** aims	**C** means	**D** intends
33	**A** so	**B** because	**C** although	**D** unless
34	**A** opposite	**B** according	**C** up	**D** due
35	**A** saved	**B** provided	**C** covered	**D** supported

WRITING

PART 1

Questions 1–5

Here are some sentences about clocks and watches.
For each question, complete the second sentence so that it means the same as the first.
Use no more than three words.
Write only the missing words on your answer sheet.
You may use this page for any rough work.

Example:

0 Clocks and watches are seen everywhere.
You can ....*see*............... **clocks and watches everywhere.**

1 The earliest clocks used the sun's shadow to tell the time.
With the earliest clocks, people .... **the time by using the sun's shadow.**

2 Modern clocks are more accurate than old-fashioned ones were.
Old-fashioned clocks weren't as .... **modern ones are.**

3 The most famous clocks in the world are made in Switzerland.
In Switzerland, they .... **the most famous clocks in the world.**

4 An alarm clock can help you wake up early.
An alarm clock is helpful .... **you need to wake up early.**

5 People without watches are often late for appointments.
People without watches are often not .... **time for appointments.**

PART 2

Question 6

You have promised to take photos at your friend Sam's 18th birthday party next week, but now you can't go to the party.

Write an e-mail to Sam. In your e-mail, you should

- explain why you can't go to the party
- apologize
- suggest someone else who can take the photos.

Write **35–45 words** on your answer sheet.

PART 3

Write an answer to **one** of the questions (**7** or **8**) in this part.

Write your answer in about **100 words** on your answer sheet.

Put the question number in the box at the top of your answer sheet.

Question 7

- This is part of a letter you receive from an English penfriend.

> I'm lucky because my school is really good and usually I love it. But some days I just hate it! What are the good and bad things about going to your school?

- Now write a letter answering your penfriend's question.
- Write your **letter** on your answer sheet.

Question 8

- Your English teacher has asked you to write a story.
- Your story must have this title:

  The message in the sand

- Write your **story** on your answer sheet.

PAPER 2 Listening Test 30 minutes (+ 6 minutes)

LISTENING

PART 1

Questions 1–7

There are seven questions in this part.
For each question there are three pictures and a short recording.
Choose the correct picture and put a tick (✓) in the box below it.

Example: Where did the man leave his sunglasses?

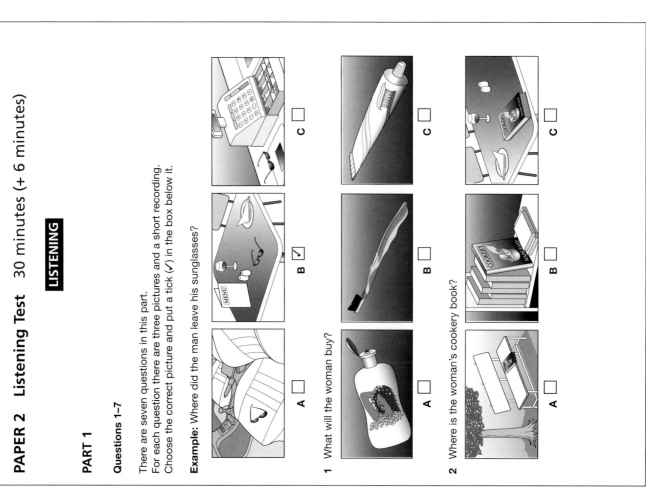

A ☐   B ✓   C ☐

1 What will the woman buy?

A ☐   B ☐   C ☐

2 Where is the woman's cookery book?

A ☐   B ☐   C ☐

3 What time will the next train for Bristol leave?

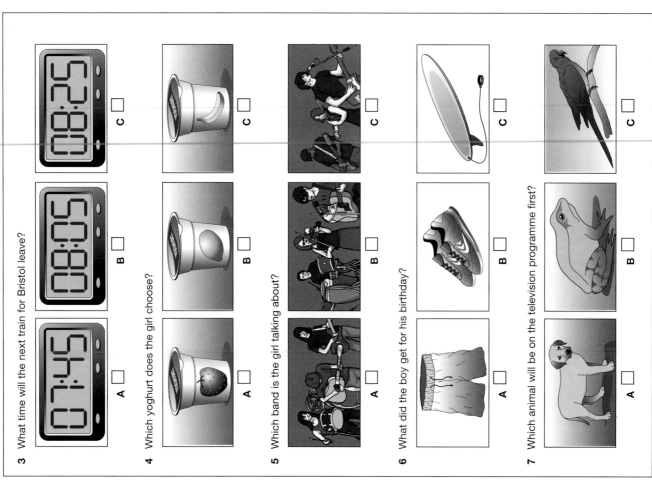

A ☐   B ☐   C ☐

4 Which yoghurt does the girl choose?

A ☐   B ☐   C ☐

5 Which band is the girl talking about?

A ☐   B ☐   C ☐

6 What did the boy get for his birthday?

A ☐   B ☐   C ☐

7 Which animal will be on the television programme first?

A ☐   B ☐   C ☐

PART 2

Questions 8–13

You will hear an interview with a woman who has written a popular novel.
For each question, put a tick (✓) in the correct box.

8 Anna's first novel was about
   A ☐ working in a school.
   B ☐ studying at a college.
   C ☐ learning to be a nurse.

9 How old was Anna when she got married?
   A ☐ 20 years old
   B ☐ 22 years old
   C ☐ 24 years old

10 An agent first liked Anna's story when
   A ☐ it was published in a magazine he read.
   B ☐ it won first prize in an Internet competition.
   C ☐ it was read out on a radio programme he heard.

11 What does Anna say about her new novel?
   A ☐ It is set in a place where she once lived.
   B ☐ It is about someone who is like her.
   C ☐ It is based on a family like hers.

12 What does Anna say about horses?
   A ☐ She would like to own one.
   B ☐ It would be fun to work with them.
   C ☐ Finding out about them was enjoyable.

13 Anna advises young writers to
   A ☐ wait until they have time to write properly.
   B ☐ keep writing even if it isn't going well.
   C ☐ spend all their free time writing.

PART 3

Questions 14–19

You will hear a student giving a talk about a person she admires.
For each question, fill in the missing information in the numbered space.

MICHAEL FOALE: SPACEMAN

Michael originally comes from **(14)** ....

Michael has spent a total of **(15)** .... in space.

Michael's first job was with a company that made **(16)** ....

Michael has to wear both a spacesuit and **(17)** .... when he walks in space.

In his most difficult space walk, Michael had to put a new **(18)** .... on a satellite.

Michael was surprised to find that the Moon is **(19)** .... in colour.

73

PART 4

Questions 20–25

Look at the six sentences for this part.

You will hear a conversation between a girl, Tanya, and a boy, Marek, about their holiday plans.

Decide if each sentence is correct or incorrect.

If it is correct, put a tick (✓) in the box under **A** for **YES**. If it is not correct, put a tick (✓) in the box under **B** for **NO**.

	A YES	B NO
20 Marek is pleased that he'll sleep in a tent on holiday.	☐	☐
21 Tanya and Marek both dislike travelling by air.	☐	☐
22 Tanya often regrets the things she buys at airports.	☐	☐
23 Tanya is going to a familiar place on holiday this year.	☐	☐
24 Marek thinks that Tanya's holiday sounds exciting.	☐	☐
25 Tanya will do some activities with her brother on holiday.	☐	☐

PAPER 3   Speaking Test   about 12 minutes

PART 1 (2–3 minutes)

The test begins with a general conversation with the examiner, who will ask you and the other candidate some questions about yourselves. Be ready to talk about your daily life, your studies, your likes and dislikes, etc. In this part, you will be asked to spell all or part of your name.

PART 2 (2–3 minutes)

The examiner says:

In the next part, you are going to talk to each other. I'm going to describe a situation to you. Your teacher has invited the whole class to a party at her house. You would like to take her a present. Talk together about the types of present you could buy, and say which would be best.

See example visual on p. 75.

PART 3 (3 minutes)

The examiner says:

Now I'd like each of you to speak on your own about something. I'm going to give each of you a photograph of people eating. Please tell us what you can see in your

See example photographs on p. 76.

PART 4 (3 minutes)

The examiner says:

Your photographs showed people eating. Now I'd like you to talk together about things you like to eat in the winter and things you like to eat in the summer.

PAPER 1 Reading and Writing Test 1 hour 30 minutes

READING

PART 1

Questions 1–5

Look at the text in each question.
What does it say?
Mark the correct letter **A**, **B** or **C** on your answer sheet.

Example:

0

These animals are dangerous. Do not cross the safety fence.

A Don't get any nearer to these animals because they may hurt you.

B Don't let these animals get out from behind this fence.

C It's dangerous to bring animals into this area.

Example answer:

Part 1			
0	A ▬	B	C

1

Wash dark colours separately at 40 °C. Dry flat away from direct sunlight.

A This mustn't be washed in water hotter than 40 °C or hung up to dry.

B This can safely be washed with white things and dried outside in the sun.

C This should be dry cleaned and not washed even at a temperature of 40 °C.

2

Karen,
This book is due back at the library today but if you want to read it, I'll get it out for another week.
Tracy

A Tracy is asking Karen if she can borrow her library book.

B Tracy is telling Karen to take her book back to the library.

C Tracy is offering to let Karen read her library book.

3

POSTC

My time spent studying Greek has been well worth it! Everyone here in this Greek village understands me although they often talk too fast for me to understand them!
Jessica

A Jessica is disappointed the Greek people can't understand her.

B Jessica feels she didn't spend enough time studying Greek.

C Jessica is pleased with her success in speaking Greek.

4

SALLY'S SANDWICHES
We're moving.
We'll welcome customers at 22 Canal Street from 7 June.

A We have already opened a new shop at a different address.

B You can't buy sandwiches in our new shop until 7 June.

C Customers will have to get their sandwiches from a different company after 7 June.

5

P **PARKING**
£2 per hour
3 hours maximum
£60 fine will be charged

A If you park here for 4 hours, you must pay a fine.

B It costs £60 to park here for 3 hours.

C Charges for parking go from £2 to £60.

PRACTICE TEST 2 – READING

PART 2

Questions 6–10

The people below are all making travel plans and want to visit the website of a travel company.

On the opposite page, there are descriptions of eight travel company websites.

Decide which website would be the most suitable for the following people.

For questions **6–10**, mark the correct letter **(A–H)** on your answer sheet.

6  Guy is a student who is planning a long trip alone through South America next year. He wants to find out more about the area, and about how he can save money, before booking anything.

7  Lenka wants to book a holiday for herself, her husband and four children on the Mediterranean coast of France. She wants to stay in a flat and hire a car.

8  Nikil has to book accommodation for 12 work colleagues who are going to London next month. He wants to use a company that has been in business for some time which will give a discount.

9 Sonia has already booked her skiing holiday in the Swiss Alps. She now needs to buy skis and boots to take with her.

10  Daniel wants to surprise his wife with tickets for a voyage on a Caribbean cruise ship. He doesn't have too much money to spend and they have to go in the next few days.

Travel Company Websites

A Best Choice

Whether you plan to travel to Europe, Asia, Africa, Australia or the Americas, we have what you need. We sell a wide range of clothing for children and adults to wear in the sun or snow, plus travel bags and all the equipment necessary for your winter sports or scuba diving holiday.

B LTC Travel

Our website is the first stop for all young, independent travellers. We give advice on travel to all parts of North and South America, including the Caribbean, and direct you towards cheap flights and low-priced accommodation. You can download free maps and country guides.

C Swift Holidays

We promise to get you the cheapest flight available to your chosen destination. We can also find you many kinds of holiday at a reduced cost if you book at the last minute. This week's special offers include a skiing holiday in the Swiss Alps and a cruise in the Caribbean.

D Go-With-Us

If you want to give your family the holiday of a lifetime, let us take care of you. Choose from a number of campsites in seaside and mountain locations throughout Europe. The price includes travel, use of a luxury tent, first-class campsite facilities, organized sporting activities and evening entertainment.

E Easy Journey

We can take the worry out of making holiday reservations. We organize group holidays (minimum size six) to a range of beautiful seaside locations around the Mediterranean and Caribbean Seas. Every sixth person in the group goes free. Stay in a three-star hotel or a holiday apartment. Car-rental included in the price.

F Faraway Tours

We offer discounts on plane fares to Asia and the Far East to students and anyone under 26. We also supply camping, mountain-climbing and sailing clothes and equipment. Travellers can exchange information, opinions and experiences in an online chat room.

G Take Off

We are a new company whose aim is to make business travel trouble-free and enjoyable. We can arrange first class tickets to anywhere in the world at a moment's notice and also make bookings at hotels with business and conference facilities. Our prices can't be beaten.

H Globetrotter

We have made travel arrangements to worldwide destinations for thirty years. We also book hotel rooms and organize car hire in all European and North American cities. We only deal with well-respected tour operators so you can be confident about our service. There are reduced prices for group bookings.

Welcome to the
Gordon Lake School of Theatre Arts

The Gordon Lake School is one of the country's leading drama schools, offering both full-time and part-time courses for those interested in a career in acting, musical theatre, directing or technical theatre.

Our permanent teaching staff are dedicated professionals who want each individual student to develop his or her skills and abilities to the full. Students also work with visiting staff who are currently earning their living in theatre, film and television.

The Gordon Lake School continues to advise students even after they have completed their studies. We run our own theatrical agency to help you find work in the profession.

Before entering the school

After we have received your application form, we will invite you to an interview and ask you to perform for us. Candidates wanting to take the acting course will have to learn and perform two pieces taken from plays. Candidates who would like to study musical theatre are required to sing two songs and take part in a dance workshop in addition to doing the two pieces from plays. Candidates are normally informed whether or not they will be offered a place on a course within two weeks of the interview.

Full-time course

After successfully completing three years of study, students receive a BA degree in performance arts. Students will be able to choose from a range of course options, depending on whether they want to concentrate on acting, musical theatre, directing or technical theatre. See our brochure for full details of these options. The aim behind all course options is to produce professionals with the ability to be regularly employed in a very varied industry.

Part-time courses

The school also offers a range of evening, weekend and summer courses for people of all ages and backgrounds These include the following:
• **Acting for the screen:** This is a two-term course on Monday evenings from 7 to 10 p.m. The first term concentrates on developing screen-acting techniques. The second term builds on this knowledge in the making of a series of short films.
• **Acting course for young people:** This five-day summer course is held every July for young people aged 12–18 who are thinking of an acting career.
• **Musical theatre course for young people:** This course is on Saturday afternoons throughout January, February and March. It is designed to train young people (11–18 years) in professional song and dance techniques. Some previous experience of dance and singing is preferred and a keen interest in performing is essential.

Applications for all part-time courses must be with us at least a month before term begins. Late applications may be considered if spaces are available.

PART 3

Questions 11–20

Look at the sentences below about a school of theatre arts.
Read the text on the opposite page to decide if each sentence is correct or incorrect.
If it is correct, mark **A** on your answer sheet.
If it is not correct, mark **B** on your answer sheet.

11 Students are sometimes taught by people from outside who are employed in the theatre.

12 Students can still get support from the school when they have finished their course.

13 At their interview, acting course candidates have to perform more than musical theatre candidates.

14 It usually takes more than two weeks before candidates hear the decision of the interviewers.

15 All students on the full-time course study the same things.

16 The full-time course is designed to qualify students for many kinds of work in the profession.

17 From the start of the 'Acting for the screen' course, students take part in films.

18 If you are 15 and want to act, you could study at the school in July.

19 It's better if young people already have some performing skills before doing the musical theatre course.

20 Applications for part-time courses should be made in the four weeks before the course begins.

PRACTICE TEST 2 – READING

PART 4

Questions 21–25

Read the text and questions below.
For each question, mark the correct letter **A**, **B**, **C** or **D** on your answer sheet.

Polly Murray, explorer

In a way, I've been an explorer all my life. My earliest memory is of a family camping holiday in Italy when I was six. We put up our tent at 4,000 metres! I remember walking down the mountain, holding my father's trousers to prevent me from falling over the rock edge. I didn't have any fear of heights then. Now I rather like looking down and feeling a bit afraid.

I spend every winter in the mountains teaching skiing. The rest of the time I go exploring. This year, I've tested out an adventure holiday in Patagonia in Argentina for a travel company and helped a TV company make a nature film in the jungle in Peru. My most exciting trip has been one I took with my friend Tania. We sailed from Greenland across Baffin Bay to Bylot Island, which is just ice, mountains and polar bears. We crossed the island on foot in seven days but, when we got to the other side, the boat wasn't there to meet us as planned. There was a terrific storm and it couldn't get to the shore, which meant we had to wait two extra days. We had run out of food and were very hungry, and very nervous about the polar bears.

To be an explorer, you need to be cool-headed. The minute you start to panic everything goes wrong, especially if you're climbing. I haven't had any serious accidents or injuries although I once had terrible toothache in Antarctica in the middle of nowhere. I just had to carry on in spite of the pain. I think I am a strong person and I can't imagine having any other kind of life.

21 What is Polly's main reason for writing this text?
A to advertise exciting holidays
B to recommend climbing as a sport
C to describe her way of life
D to encourage people to travel

22 What happened to Polly at the age of six?
A She went camping in the mountains.
B She fell when she was mountain climbing.
C She became frightened of high mountains.
D She and her father got lost in the mountains.

23 Polly couldn't leave Bylot Island when she wanted to because
A polar bears stopped her from crossing the ice.
B she was too weak and hungry to travel.
C she was waiting in the wrong place for her boat.
D bad weather prevented her boat from reaching her.

24 According to Polly, a good explorer is someone who
A avoids accidents and injuries.
B learns from bad experiences.
C is able to climb difficult mountains.
D can stay calm in any situation.

25 Which person is talking about Polly?

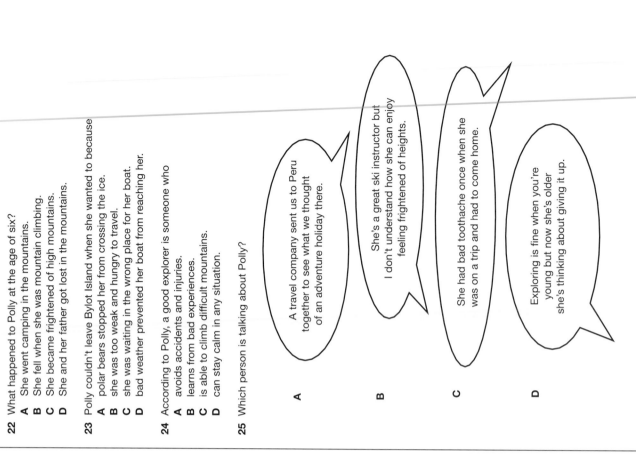

A A travel company sent us to Peru together to see what we thought of an adventure holiday there.

B She's a great ski instructor but I don't understand how she can enjoy feeling frightened of heights.

C She had bad toothache once when she was on a trip and had to come home.

D Exploring is fine when you're young but now she's older she's thinking about giving it up.

PART 5

Questions 26–35

Read the text below and choose the correct word for each space.
For each question, mark the correct letter **A**, **B**, **C** or **D** on your answer sheet.

Example:

| 0 | **A** results | **B** decisions | **C** effects | **D** events |

```
        Part 5
   0 | A   B   C   D
       ▬   □   □   □
```

WOMEN MAKE THE BEST DRIVERS

In London, only one in ten bus drivers is a women. Yet, according to the **(0)**..... of recent research, women are better at **(26)**..... with problem passengers, have fewer accidents and are quicker at learning to drive buses than men.

Connie Wilson **(27)**..... a bus driver a year ago. '**(28)**..... first, driving a bus was quite frightening,' she says. 'I had no idea of the size of the vehicle or **(29)**..... to handle it. But after seven weeks of training, I passed the test first time. Trying to **(30)**..... to the timetable when the traffic is **(31)**..... isn't easy but I like the challenge! Some passengers **(32)**..... be rude, especially if they've had to **(33)**..... a long time for the bus. But most are pleased to have a woman driver. There's no **(34)**..... why women can't do the job just as well as men. I'd **(35)**..... it to any woman.'

26	**A** managing	**B** dealing	**C** considering	**D** behaving
27	**A** got	**B** started	**C** turned	**D** became
28	**A** At	**B** By	**C** In	**D** From
29	**A** what	**B** which	**C** why	**D** how
30	**A** check	**B** respect	**C** keep	**D** carry
31	**A** deep	**B** large	**C** heavy	**D** rough
32	**A** can	**B** should	**C** need	**D** want
33	**A** delay	**B** wait	**C** expect	**D** attend
34	**A** cause	**B** reason	**C** purpose	**D** account
35	**A** approve	**B** lead	**C** recommend	**D** admire

PART 1

Questions 1–5

Here are some sentences about the alphabet.
For each question, complete the second sentence so that it means the same as the first.
Use no more than three words.
Write only the missing words on your answer sheet.
You may use this page for any rough work.

Example: The alphabet we use in English has 26 letters.
In the alphabet we use in English, ..._there_..... .... are 26 letters.

1 The two Greek letters 'alpha' and 'beta' give us the word 'alphabet'.
We get the word 'alphabet' .... **the two Greek letters 'alpha' and 'beta'.**

2 An alphabet was first used about 3,500 years ago.
People .... **an alphabet for about 3,500 years.**

3 Without an alphabet, we couldn't write down our ideas.
If we .... **have an alphabet, we couldn't write down our ideas.**

4 You can't learn to read and write until you know your alphabet.
You must know your alphabet .... **you can learn to read and write.**

5 Is learning the alphabet easier for children than learning to count?
Is learning to count not .... **for children as learning the alphabet?**

PART 2

Question 6

An English family has moved into the apartment next door to you, and you'd like to introduce yourself to them.

Write a note to the family. In your note, you should

- introduce yourself
- give them a piece of useful information about the neighbourhood
- offer to do something for the family.

Write **35–45 words** on your answer sheet.

PART 3

Write an answer to **one** of the questions (**7** or **8**) in this part.
Write your answer in about **100 words** on your answer sheet.
Mark the question number in the box at the top of your answer sheet.

Question 7

- This is part of a letter you receive from an English penfriend.

> *I'm planning to visit your country soon. Where should I go?
> I'm interested in history, beautiful scenery and anything
> you recommend.*

- Now write a letter to tell your penfriend about places to visit in your country.
- Write your **letter** on your answer sheet.

Question 8

- Your English teacher has asked you to write a story.
- Your story must begin with this sentence:

> *Emma didn't know how to find the money she needed.*

- Write your **story** on your answer sheet.

PAPER 2   Listening Test   30 minutes (+ 6 minutes)

LISTENING

PART 1

Questions 1–7

There are seven questions in this part.
For each question there are three pictures and a short recording.
Choose the correct picture and put a tick (✓) in the box below it.

Example: Where did the man leave his sunglasses?

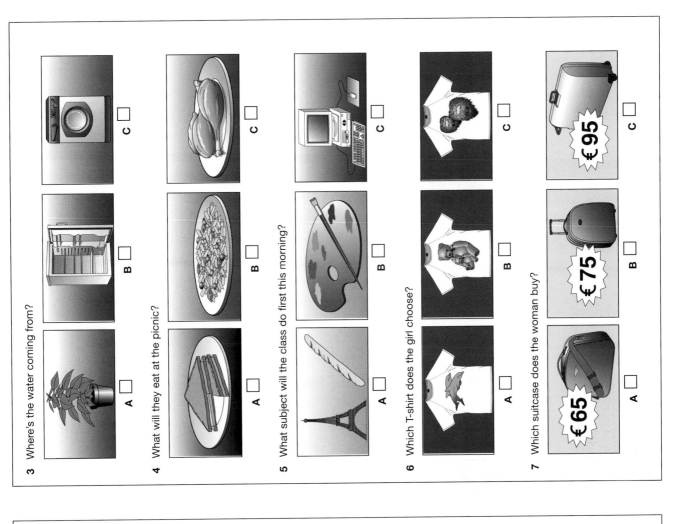

1 Where will they go on holiday?

2 What are they cleaning?

3 Where's the water coming from?

4 What will they eat at the picnic?

5 What subject will the class do first this morning?

6 Which T-shirt does the girl choose?

7 Which suitcase does the woman buy?

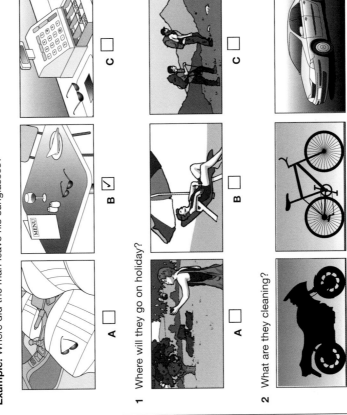

€ 65   € 75   € 95

PRACTICE TEST 2 – LISTENING

PART 2

Questions 8–13

You will hear an interview with Stella Brady who is a professional photographer.
For each question, put a tick (✓) in the correct box.

8 Stella first won a photography
competition when she was

A ☐ eight years old.
B ☐ ten years old.
C ☐ twelve years old.

9 Stella first learnt about
photography from

A ☐ her parents.
B ☐ her uncle.
C ☐ her brother.

10 What did Stella do when she
left school?

A ☐ She got a job to make some money.
B ☐ She went on holiday before starting work.
C ☐ She did some training in photography.

11 What does Stella say about
Australia?

A ☐ She didn't enjoy taking photos there.
B ☐ She learnt a lot about photography there.
C ☐ She found lots of work as a photographer
there.

12 In Stella's studio, you can
mostly see

A ☐ photos of weddings.
B ☐ sports photography.
C ☐ artistic photographs.

13 In the future, Stella plans to

A ☐ try a new kind of photography.
B ☐ take photographs of works of art.
C ☐ start painting people instead.

PART 3

Questions 14-19

You will hear a tour guide talking to some visitors in a jewellery workshop.
For each question, fill in the missing information in the numbered space.

JEWELLERY WORKSHOP

Where many of the artists
come from: (14) ....

The metal they use most: (15) ....

What they use instead of stones: (16) .... or seeds

What the artist thinks of first: the (17) .... of the piece

Where many of the artists get
their ideas: from (18) ....

Where people wear the workshop's
best-known jewellery: in their (19) ....

PAPER 3   Speaking Test   about 12 minutes

PART 1 (2–3 minutes)

The test begins with a general conversation with the examiner, who will ask you and the other candidate some questions about yourselves. Be ready to talk about your daily life, your studies, your likes and dislikes, etc. In this part, you will be asked to spell all or part of your name.

PART 2 (2–3 minutes)

The examiner says:

In the next part you will talk to each other. I'm going to describe a situation to you. A group of teenagers from Australia is coming to spend a week in this country in the spring. They have asked what things they need to bring with them. Talk together about the different things they should bring and say which will be the most useful.

See example visual on p. 86.

PART 3 (3 minutes)

The examiner says:

Now I'd like each of you to talk on your own about something. I'm going to give each of you a photograph of people studying. Please tell us what you can see in your photograph.

See example photographs on p. 87.

PART 4 (3 minutes)

The examiner says:

Your photographs showed people studying. Now I'd like you to talk together about where you go when you want to study, and the best time of day for studying.

PART 4

Questions 20–25

Look at the six sentences for this part.
You will hear a conversation between a boy, Darren, and a girl, Monica, about a football match.
Decide if each sentence is correct or incorrect.
If it is correct, put a tick (✓) in the box under **A** for **YES**. If it is not correct, put a tick (✓) in the box under **B** for **NO**.

	A YES	B NO
20 Monica remembers seeing Darren at the football match.	☐	☐
21 Monica admits this was the first match she's ever been to.	☐	☐
22 Monica's friends were surprised by the size of the stadium.	☐	☐
23 Darren and Monica agree that going to a match is expensive.	☐	☐
24 Monica was disappointed by the match itself.	☐	☐
25 Darren thinks that the local team played well enough to win.	☐	☐

Unit 6

Vocabulary

1 Match the items (1–10) to the places where you can buy them (a–j).

1	magazine	a	gift shop
2	medicine	b	travel agent's
3	meat	c	baker's
4	bread	d	box office
5	souvenir	e	chemist's
6	petrol	f	post office
7	plane ticket	g	service station
8	stamp	h	garden centre
9	plant	i	newsagent's
10	theatre ticket	j	butcher's

2 Which of the items (1–10) could you also buy:

- on the Internet?
- in a supermarket?

3 Reorder the letters to make adjectives.

1	ritdy	6	ppayh ......
2	pemyt	7	nigrob ......
3	yonis	8	cixedet ......
4	saye	9	dure ......
5	chir	10	daxerel ......

4 Match the adjectives above to their opposites (a–j) below.

a	quiet	f	difficult
b	sad	g	poor
c	full	h	interesting
d	calm	i	polite
e	stressed	j	clean

Grammar

5 Complete the sentences with *some* or *any*.

1 Have you got ...... brothers or sisters?
2 Would you like ...... cake with your coffee?
3 There aren't ...... red peppers left, I'm afraid, only green ones.
4 Could you give me ...... information about computer games, please?
5 Have you seen ...... good films lately?
6 There isn't ...... milk in the fridge. Have we run out?
7 I'd like to buy ...... apples, please.
8 Would you like ...... black pepper on your pizza?

Unit 7

Vocabulary

1 Underline the word in each group which does not belong.

1 fry boil roast peel bake
2 cucumber melon orange sausage strawberry
3 bowl pastry pan cup dish
4 duck lamb steak turkey mushroom
5 soup lemonade onion juice milk
6 dessert snack picnic barbecue lunch

2 What is each person doing? Choose a word from the box.

apologising	warning	regretting promising
agreeing	disagreeing	offering
complaining	suggesting	refusing

1 'I'm sorry I missed your party. I was ill.'
2 'I'll carry that bag for you if you like.'
3 'No thank you, I had one a few minutes ago.'
4 'I wish I hadn't said that Anne's hair looked funny.'
5 'You made a lot of noise last night. I couldn't get off to sleep.'
6 'I will remember to post your letter, honestly.'
7 'Why don't we go to the cinema this evening?'
8 'You're right – we should tell our parents where we're going.'
9 'Be careful. That water's very hot.'
10 'I'm sorry, but I don't think that's such a good idea.'

Grammar

3 Complete the gap in the second sentence using reported speech.

1 'Don't eat any more biscuits, Harry,' said his mother.
Harry's mother told him not .... biscuits.
2 'Boil the rice for forty minutes,' said the cookery teacher to her class.
The cookery teacher told her class .... for forty minutes.
3 'Don't burn the sauce, Diana,' said her father.
Diana's father told .... the sauce.
4 'Open the door for me please, Cathy,' said her sister.
Cathy's sister asked .... door.
5 'What are we having for dinner, Mum?' asked Tom.
Tom asked his mum what .... dinner.

Unit 8

Vocabulary

1 Reorder the words to make names of animals.

1	drib	5	bartib ......
2	gerti	6	meykon ......
3	derspi	7	toga ......
4	krash	8	noil ......

2 Write an adjective in each space by adding a suffix to the words in bold.

1 I like to see the ...... way of life in the places I visit. **tradition**
2 If you take that path up the mountain, you'll see a ...... waterfall. **wonder**
3 We spent a ...... afternoon relaxing by a lake. **please**
4 The best part of my trip was seeing the ...... scenery. **amaze**
5 There were a ...... number of tourists in such a remote area. **surprise**
6 I felt ...... when I tried to speak the local language. **embarrass**

Grammar

3 Choose the correct verb form.

1 I *am learning/learn* English at the moment.
2 I usually *am swimming/swim* in the sea in the summer.
3 We never *going/go* away on holiday because we have three dogs.
4 Do you *working/work* at the weekend?
5 Do you enjoy *reading/read* magazines?
6 Tammy *is getting/gets* up at seven o'clock every morning.
7 Connie *is having/has* a large wardrobe in her bedroom.
8 I don't like my bedroom *being/is* untidy.

Unit 9

Vocabulary

1 How many words can you find in the wordsquare? Complete the sentences with the words you find.

Across

1 ...... is the most popular water sport.
2 Athletes are trained by a ....
3 Going for a ...... around the park is a good way of keeping fit.
4 Table ...... is also known as *ping pong*.
5 Many simple games use a ...... and a ball.
6 To win at sport, you need a good level of ....
7 You wear ...... to move quickly over snow.

Down

1 Footballers usually wear a pair of ....
2 Playing ...... usually involves a long walk.
3 You wear a ...... for underwater sports.
4 ...... is a team game played on a frozen surface.
5 ...... is a type of football that uses an oval ball.
6 You have to get the ball over a ...... in volleyball.
7 ...... involves hitting a ball against a wall.
8 The winner of a race usually wins a ....
9 To win a football match, a team must score at least one ....
10 Most athletes wear a ...... when they're training.

S	W	I	M	M	I	N	G	T
H	E	C	O	A	C	H	P	R
O	T	E	N	N	I	S	R	A
R	S	H	R	U	N	Q	I	C
T	U	O	U	K	E	U	Z	K
S	I	C	G	J	T	A	E	S
G	T	K	B	A	T	S	G	U
O	N	E	Y	X	J	H	O	I
L	N	Y	S	K	I	S	A	T
F	I	T	N	E	S	S	L	J

2 Match (1–10) to (a–h) to make the names of health problems. Some words in a–h can be used more than once.

1	head	a	throat
2	sore	b	arm
3	broken	c	ache
4	high	d	finger
5	cut	e	sick
6	ear	f	ankle
7	tooth	g	nose
8	feel	h	temperature
9	twisted		
10	runny		

Grammar

3 Complete the sentences with *if* or *unless*.

1 I don't go out ...... I've finished my homework.
2 ...... you lend me your new CD, I'll help you with your maths.
3 I won't go out ...... it stops raining because I don't want to get wet.
4 You shouldn't play sports ...... you have a temperature.
5 ...... you train hard, you can't hope to become a top sportsperson.
6 ...... we're lucky, we should arrive just in time to see the match.

Unit 10

Vocabulary

1 Write a noun in each space by adding a suffix to the words in bold.

1 I went to see an ...... of modern art. **exhibit**
2 I think there are too many ...... on television. **advertise**
3 The price for ...... to the theme park is quite high. **admit**
4 Have you got an Internet ...... in your hotel room? **connect**
5 I'm going to see the latest film by my favourite .... **direct**
6 I think e-mail is the easiest form of .... **communicate**
7 We have quite a lot of electrical ...... in our classroom. **equip**
8 The singer gave an excellent ...... at the concert. **perform**

Grammar

2 Complete the sentences with the correct words.

1 I think that text messaging is more fun ...... e-mailing.
2 I prefer watching a DVD ...... going to the cinema.
3 Who does this Mp3 player belong ...... ?
4 If I were you, I'd get a more ...... to date computer.
5 I ...... afford to buy a new printer until next month.
6 Tony is borrowing a digital camera ...... his brother.
7 I ...... a headache if I look at a screen for too long.
8 It was ...... a cold evening that they decided to stay in and watch television.

Irregular verbs

present	past simple	past participle
be	was/were	been
beat	beat	beaten
become	became	become
begin	began	begun
bend	bent	bent
bite	bit	bitten
bleed	bled	bled
blow	blew	blown
break	broke	broken
bring	brought	brought
build	built	built
burn	burnt	burnt
buy	bought	bought
catch	caught	caught
choose	chose	chosen
come	came	come
cost	cost	cost
cut	cut	cut
dig	dug	dug
do	did	done
draw	drew	drawn
dream	dreamt	dreamt
drink	drank	drunk
drive	drove	driven
eat	ate	eaten
fall	fell	fallen
feed	fed	fed
feel	felt	felt
fight	fought	fought
find	found	found
fly	flew	flown
forget	forgot	forgotten
forgive	forgave	forgiven
freeze	froze	frozen
get	got	got
give	gave	given
go	went	gone
grow	grew	grown
have	had	had
hear	heard	heard
hide	hid	hidden
hit	hit	hit
hold	held	held
hurt	hurt	hurt
keep	kept	kept
know	knew	known
lay	laid	laid
lead	led	led

present	past simple	past participle
learn	learnt	learnt
leave	left	left
lend	lent	lent
let	let	let
lie	lay	lain
light	lit	lit
lose	lost	lost
make	made	made
mean	meant	meant
meet	met	met
pay	paid	paid
put	put	put
read	read	read
ride	rode	ridden
ring	rang	rung
rise	rose	risen
run	ran	run
say	said	said
see	saw	seen
sell	sold	sold
send	sent	sent
set	set	set
shake	shook	shaken
shine	shone	shone
shoot	shot	shot
show	showed	shown
shut	shut	shut
sing	sang	sung
sit	sat	sat
sleep	slept	slept
smell	smelt	smelt
speak	spoke	spoken
spell	spelt	spelt
spend	spent	spent
spread	spread	spread
stand	stood	stood
steal	stole	stolen
sweep	swept	swept
swim	swam	swum
take	took	taken
teach	taught	taught
tear	tore	torn
tell	told	told
think	thought	thought
throw	threw	thrown
wake	woke	woken
wear	wore	worn
win	won	won
write	wrote	written

Keys to Units 1–10

1 1 Personal information

2 Listening 🔘 1.1 (page 6)

1

A
Name: John
Surname: Rose
Home town: London
E-mail address: john@webmail.net
Mobile number: 02227 813000
Sex: Male
Age: 16
Interests: Football, tennis, volleyball, listening to music, watching television

B
Name: Amanda
Surname: Wilson
Home town: York
E-mail address: amanda@webmail.net
Mobile number: 02227 963214
Sex: Female
Age: 17
Interests: Horse riding, hill walking, getting out of the city

3 Speaking 🔘 1.2 (page 7)

3
1   Yolanda Brown
2   Yusuf Amiri
3   Angela Beaufort
4   Paolo Mitchell
5   Irina Gallagher

4 Writing (page 7)

1   good football
2   interested in
3   old are
4   do you
5   you spell

6 Listening 🔘 1.3 (page 8)

1   1 C   2 E   3 F   4 B   5 G

2   A/D

7 Reading (page 8)

1   1 B   2 C

1 2 A regular thing

1 Vocabulary (page 9)

1
attend: class, meeting
boil: water
brush: hair, pet, shoes, teeth
clean: desk, furniture, shoes, teeth
comb: hair
dial: number
dust: desk, furniture
feed: pet
iron: shirt
miss: bus, class, meeting
tidy: desk, dishes, hair
tie: hair, shoelaces
wash: dishes, hair, pet, shirt

2
hand in: books, homework
join in: game
plug in: light, radio
put away: books, game, homework, make-up, socks, umbrella
put on: light, make-up, music, radio, socks
put up: umbrella
take off: make-up, socks
turn on: light, music, radio
turn up: light, music, radio

2 Reading (page 9)

1 A, B   2 C   3 A   4 C   5 A   6 B, C
7 B   8 A

4 Writing (page 11)

1   as tidy as
2   faster than
3   more comfortable than
4   less homework than
5   worse than

5 Reading (page 11)

2
1 A   2 B   3 D   4 A   5 C   6 C   7 B
8 D   9 A   10 B

Key to Practice Test 1

Paper 1 Reading and Writing

Page 66 Reading PART 1
1 A 2 C 3 B 4 B 5 C

Page 67 Reading PART 2
6 F 7 B 8 D 9 H 10 C

Page 68 Reading PART 3
11 A 12 B 13 A 14 B 15 B
16 B 17 A 18 B 19 A 20 B

Page 69 Reading PART 4
21 D 22 B 23 C 24 A 25 C

Page 70 Reading PART 5
26 B 27 C 28 A 29 A 30 D
31 D 32 C 33 B 34 B 35 A

Page 70 Writing PART 1
1 told / could tell
2 accurate as
3 make
4 if/when/whenever
5 on

Page 71 Writing PART 2
There are 5 marks for this part. To get 5 marks, the answer should include these points:

- a reason for not being able to go to the party
- an apology for not being able to go to the party
- the name of someone else who can take the photos.

More information about how this part is assessed is given on pages 121–124.

Page 71 Writing PART 3
There are 15 marks for this part.
Information about how this part is assessed is given on pages 121–124.

Paper 2 Listening

Page 72 Listening PART 1
1 B 2 B 3 C 4 C 5 C 6 B 7 A

Page 73 Listening PART 2
8 A 9 B 10 C 11 A 12 C 13 B

Page 73 Listening PART 3
14 England
15 374 days
16 (aero/air)planes
17 gloves
18 computer
19 brown

Page 74 Listening PART 4
20 B 21 B 22 A 23 B 24 A 25 B

Key to Practice Test 2

Paper 1 Reading and Writing

Page 77 Reading PART 1
1 A   2 C   3 C   4 B   5 A

Page 78 Reading PART 2
6 B   7 E   8 H   9 A   10 C

Page 79 Reading PART 3
11 A   12 A   13 B   14 B   15 B
16 A   17 B   18 A   19 A   20 B

Page 80 Reading PART 4
21 C   22 A   23 D   24 D   25 B

Page 81 Reading PART 5
26 B   27 D   28 A   29 D   30 C
31 C   32 A   33 B   34 B   35 C

Page 81 Writing PART 1
1   from
2   have used
3   didn't/did not
4   before
5   as easy/so easy

Page 82 Writing PART 2
There are 5 marks for this part. To get 5 marks, the answer should include these points:

• some information introducing self
• a piece of useful information about the neighbourhood
• an offer to do something for the family

More information about how this part is assessed is given on pages 121–124.

Page 82 Writing PART 3
There are 15 marks for this part.
Information about how this part is assessed is given on pages 121–124.

Paper 2 Listening

Page 83 Listening PART 1
1 A   2 C   3 C   4 B   5 C   6 A   7 B

Page 84 Listening PART 2
8 C   9 B   10 A   11 B   12 C   13 A

Page 84 Listening PART 3
14   Africa
15   gold
16   shells
17   shape
18   music
19   hair

Page 85 Listening PART 4
20 A   21 B   22 B   23 B   24 A   25 A

Grammar and vocabulary practice key

Unit 1

Exercise 1
1 up
2 on
3 up
4 off
5 on
6 on
7 out

Exercise 2
Across
1 sock
2 rubber
3 shower
4 ruler
5 shelf
6 towel
7 comb
8 soap

Down
1 toothbrush
2 scissors
3 watch
4 sheet
5 pencil
6 lamp
7 car
8 shampoo

Unit 2

Exercise 1
1 bookshop
2 romance
3 imagination
4 educated
5 met
6 done
7 much

Exercise 2
1 in
2 with
3 to
4 on
5 on

Unit 3

Exercise 1
1 too much
2 a lot of
3 too
4 enough
5 very

Exercise 2
pilot – aeroplane
dentist – surgery
hairdresser – salon
judge – court
lecturer – college
engineer – factory
secretary – office
sales assistant – shop
waiter – restaurant
presenter – TV station
nurse – hospital
footballer – stadium
priest – church
fisherman – ship
farmer – farm

Exercise 3
1 hairdresser
2 waiter
3 nurse
4 fisherman
5 secretary
6 presenter
7 farmer
8 footballer

Unit 4

Exercise 1
1d   9m
2g   10f
3k   11j
4i   12l
5n   13o
6b   14e
7a   15c
8h

Exercise 2
1 all rooms
2 bedroom
3 sitting room
4 bedroom/ sitting room
5 all rooms
6 kitchen
7 sitting room/ bedroom
8 kitchen
9 all rooms
10 kitchen
11 dining room
12 bathroom
13 bathroom
14 kitchen
15 all rooms

Exercise 3
1 impatient
2 unattractive
3 disappeared
4 Unfortunately, impossible
5 incorrectly
6 unable
7 disadvantage

Exercise 4
1 furniture
2 information
3 hair
4 spaghetti
5 coffees

Unit 5

Exercise 1
Across
1 carpark
2 map
3 lands
4 delays
5 passport
6 traffic
7 via

Down
1 check in
2 arrivals
3 rail
4 port
5 stop
6 route
7 visa
8 luggage

Exercise 2
1 by
2 on
3 on
4 out
5 off
6 in
7 up
8 slow

Unit 6

Exercise 1
1i   6g
2e   7b
3j   8f
4c   9h
5a   10d

Exercise 2
Internet: all except petrol and stamps
Supermarket: all

Exercise 3
1 dirty
2 empty
3 noisy
4 easy
5 rich
6 happy
7 boring
8 excited
9 rude
10 relaxed

Exercise 4
1 j   6 b
2 c   7 h
3 a   8 d
4 f   9 i
5 g   10 e

Exercise 5
1 any
2 some
3 any
4 some
5 any
6 any
7 some
8 some

Unit 7

Exercise 1
1 peel
2 sausage
3 pastry
4 mushroom
5 onion
6 dessert

Exercise 2
1 apologising
2 offering
3 refusing
4 regretting
5 complaining
6 promising
7 suggesting
8 agreeing
9 warning
10 disagreeing

Exercise 3
1 to eat any more
2 to boil the rice
3 her not to burn
4 her to open the
5 they were having for

Unit 8

Exercise 1
1 bird
2 tiger
3 spider
4 shark
5 rabbit
6 monkey
7 goat
8 lion

Exercise 2
1 traditional
2 wonderful
3 pleasant
4 amazing
5 surprising
6 embarrassed

Exercise 3
1 am learning
2 swim
3 go
4 work
5 reading
6 gets
7 has
8 being

Unit 9

Exercise 1
Across
1 Swimming
2 coach
3 run
4 tennis
5 bat
6 fitness
7 skis

Down
1 shorts
2 golf
3 wetsuit
4 Ice hockey
5 Rugby
6 net
7 Squash
8 prize
9 goal
10 tracksuit

Exercise 2
1c headache
2a sore throat
3b broken arm
4h high temperature
5d cut finger
6c earache
7c toothache
8e feel sick
9f twisted ankle
10g runny nose

Exercise 3
1 unless
2 If
3 unless
4 if
5 Unless
6 If

Unit 10

Exercise 1
1 exhibition
2 advertisements
3 admission
4 connection
5 director
6 communication
7 equipment
8 performance

Exercise 2
1 than
2 to
3 to
4 up
5 can't/cannot
6 from
7 get
8 such

Recording scripts for Units 1–10

1 1 Personal information

2 Listening 1.1 (page 6)

1

A Hello. My name is John, that's J-O-H-N. And my surname is Rose, that's R-O-S-E. I would like to give you some information about myself. First of all, I live in London and my e-mail address is: john@webmail.net. Or you can get me on my mobile, the number is: 02227 813000. So, what else can I tell you? I'm a 16-year-old boy and so I'm still at school and I'm very interested in sport. I'm quite good at football and I also enjoy playing tennis and volleyball. When I'm not playing sport, I like listening to music and watching television.

B Hello. My name's Amanda Wilson and you spell my first name A-M-A-N-D-A, Amanda, and my surname is Wilson, which is spelt W-I-L-S-O-N. My name's not really difficult to spell, but people always seem to make mistakes in it! I live in York, that's Y-O-R-K and my e-mail address is: amanda@webmail.net. I've got a mobile phone, but I don't use it that much. The number is: 02227 963214. So, what can I tell you about myself? Well, I'm a 17-year-old English girl and I work as a shop assistant in a large shop in my home city. In my free time, I like to get out of the city, however, and I'm very interested in horse riding and hill walking. I'm not very good at horse riding yet because I only started last year, but I've been hill walking since I was 12 years old. I love it!

3 Speaking 1.2 (page 7)

3

1 My name is Yolanda Brown. That's YOLANDA BROWN.
2 My name is Yusuf Amiri. That's YUSUF AMIRI.
3 My name is Angela Beaufort. That's ANGELA BEAUFORT.
4 My name is Paolo Mitchell. That's PAOLO MITCHELL.
5 My name is Irina Gallagher. That's IRINA GALLAGHER.

6 Listening 1.3 (page 8)

2

David: Hello. I'm David.
Victoria: Hi. I'm Victoria. I'm a friend of Tom's from college.
David: Yes, I'm one of his friends too, and we play football together. What do you study?
Victoria: I'm doing languages. What about you?
David: I've finished college, actually, and I'm working as a windsurfing instructor.
Victoria: Oh, I'm really interested in watersports, but I'm not very good at windsurfing.
David: That doesn't matter. You could learn.
Victoria: Yes, I suppose so. But what I'm really interested in is sailing.
David: So am I. I'm running a course which starts next week. Would you be interested in joining?
Victoria: Oh … I might be … it depends.

2 1 You live and learn

2 Speaking 🔊 1.4 (page 12)

2

Boy: Hello, Polly. How are your Spanish classes going?

Polly: Oh, OK. The teacher's very nice, but the classes are a bit boring. I really like studying on my own, you know. My dad bought me a Spanish CD for my computer, but actually I prefer the textbook because I'm good at grammar, and the book has got lots of practice exercises. One day, I'd like to be able to listen and understand the words to Spanish pop music, but I'm not good enough for that yet!

3 Speaking 🔊 1.5 (page 14)

3

Valerie: So, our friend wants to learn a new language?

Pietro: That's right, and he's only got £20 to spend, so he can't buy all these things, can he?

Valerie: No, he can't. Let's start by talking about which of them will be useful for him.

Pietro: OK, then afterwards we can decide which one he should buy.

Valerie: OK. Shall we start with this one, the dictionary?

Pietro: Yes, I think he should buy one of those, because it's very useful if you don't know what words mean.

Valerie: Yes, I agree, and it's also good for checking spelling. But what about a textbook? They're useful too.

Pietro: Yes they are, but maybe he won't need one because he'll have a teacher.

Valerie: Possibly. Or he may get one free when he pays for the course.

Pietro: Oh yes, that's a good point.

4 Listening 🔊 1.6 (page 14)

Tim: Hi Janet. How's your computer course going?

Janet: Oh, I've just had my class, actually. We have them twice a week and each one lasts two hours.

Tim: Gosh. That's long. Doesn't it get boring?

Janet: Well, you need that long to actually do a whole document. It's really good because I can do all sorts of things on my computer that I never even knew existed before.

Tim: I can't say the same for my cookery course.

Janet: Oh, Tim, why not? I thought you were enjoying it.

Tim: Oh it's enjoyable enough, but we just don't seem to make much progress. We spent the whole of last week's lesson learning how to fry an egg.

Janet: Well, it's not an easy thing to do properly, you know.

Tim: Oh I know, but I don't even like eggs.

Janet: Oh poor Tim! So … how often is it?

Tim: Just once a week, for an hour and a half.

Janet: And do you get to eat all the things you make?

Tim: Well, you're not meant to eat them there, but you can take them home because you have to buy all the stuff in the first place. It's cakes next week.

Janet: Oh, that sounds fun!

Tim: Oh yes. I'm looking forward to it. But Janet, I wanted to ask you something, actually. Have you learnt how to send e-mails on your course yet?

Janet: Oh yes, we did that in the first week.

Tim: Because I can't get my computer to send them properly, and I was wondering if you'd show me how it's done?

Janet: Well, if you bring me one of your cakes, I suppose I could try.

Tim: Great, well, when I've made them …

3 2 Just the job

3 Listening 🔊 1.7–10 **(page 22)**

1

1

I love what I do and I'm very proud of the uniform I wear. I drive around for most of the day but I'm always somewhere in the city centre. My job is controlling the traffic. When I hear there's a traffic problem I go and see what I can do about it. I just use my hands and my voice – no equipment's necessary – except for my car, of course. I couldn't work without that!

2

I never did well at school. I was only interested in drawing – I was quite good at that. And that's what I do now – drawing. I work in an advertising agency and I do the artwork for advertisements. But I don't use a pencil or paint – it's all done on a computer – that's the only piece of equipment I need. I like being comfortable when I work, so I wear jeans. I don't even own a suit.

3

This is my first job and I've only been here for a year. My microscope is my most important piece of equipment. I couldn't do my work here in the zoo without it. I love animals but I don't often get to see the ones here! My job is testing. I test all kinds of things – the animals' food, the water they drink, and if they get ill, I test their blood. It's very important that everything here is clean, so I have to wear a white coat over my clothes, and I'm always washing my hands!

4

Actually, I want to change what I do. I work in a bank, and it's a good job, but I'd like to do something more exciting. Here it's the same thing every day. My job is helping customers. I help customers when they come into the bank and I help them when they phone up. I don't really have any equipment apart from the phone. I spend a lot of time on the phone. I have to wear a suit at work, which I hate – I'd much prefer to wear jeans!

2 🔊 1.11

Presenter: ... and today in our series about people who work for themselves, we have Amanda Turner. Good morning, Amanda. Tell us what you do.

Amanda: Well, basically I'm a cook. Unlike most cooks, who work at home or in a restaurant, I'm employed by various recording studios. When musicians are making an album, they have to stay in the studio all day, so I go there and prepare meals for them.

Presenter: Are musicians hard to please?

Amanda: Fortunately, they seem to be satisfied with what I do. When they're recording, they want something tasty but quite simple. They don't want to eat a lot, or be given unfamiliar dishes. The food has to be good for them because they're always worried about getting ill, or putting on weight.

Presenter: Would you call it a stressful job?

Amanda: It isn't usually. I only get worried when they forget to tell me how many people will want to eat, or when they tell me to expect five for a meal and then fifteen hungry people arrive! Often I don't have a proper kitchen to work in, and sometimes the meal is ready long before the musicians have finished playing. But I don't mind that.

Presenter: You're happy in your work, then?

Amanda: Oh, yes. I know I'm lucky to do what I enjoy, and to get paid well for it. And I meet all sorts of interesting people! Think of your favourite boy band, and I've probably cooked them a meal! But I work with all kinds of musicians, pop and classical, famous and unknown, young and old. I'm happiest when I'm cooking for the young ones. They always *really* enjoy my food and say nice things about it.

Presenter: So how long is a typical day?

Amanda: *Very* long! I walk round the market early in the morning, buying vegetables and fresh meat and fish. I have to be at the studios by noon. I don't drive, and anyway it's always difficult to park, so they send a car to pick me up. Going on the bus with all my bags of shopping would be terrible! After cooking, serving and clearing up, I never get home before nine in the evening. My daughter prepares a snack for us while I tell her about the day's music. I also do a cookery page for a monthly magazine, so before I go to bed, I do some work on that. I always sleep really well!

Presenter: It sounds like a busy life! Thanks for talking to us, Amanda.

4 1 House and home

3 **Listening** 1.12 **(page 25)**

1

In my room, there's not much furniture. I've got a bed, of course, but I don't have a wardrobe because I keep all my clothes in a chest of drawers. My parents don't like me putting posters on the wall, and for a long time I didn't have any, but I've recently been allowed to put up one or two. My parents bought me a desk to do my homework on, but I don't use it much. I like my room. It's nice.

5 **Listening** 1.13–16 **(page 26)**

1

Boy: Mum, I can't find my mobile phone. It isn't on my bedside table.

Mum: Well, I haven't touched it. You sometimes put it in your drawer or perhaps it's still in the pocket of the jacket you were wearing last night. It's hanging up by the door.

Boy: No, I used it after I came in, and I was in my bedroom.

Mum: Well, you obviously still had your jacket on because it's in the pocket like I said.

Boy: Oh right.

2

And now a change to our schedule for this afternoon. The film, *Man of Destiny* will not now begin at 3.45 as advertised. This is because there will be an extended edition of the news to report on today's exciting events in the athletics championships. The film will now be shown at 4.35. You can, however, still see the weather forecast at the normal time of 3.35.

3

Man: Would you like to order, Madam? The soup of the day is mushroom, served with garlic bread.

Woman: Oh, it's too hot for soup, but I want more than a salad. What do you suggest?

Man: Well, the fish is very good – that comes with either chips or a salad.

Woman: I see. Perhaps I'll just have a salad after all – I had some lovely fish for lunch, so perhaps I don't need so much this evening actually.

4

Woman: Hello, I've come to cut Susie's hair for her.

Man: Oh yes, come in. She's expecting you.

Woman: I wasn't sure what to bring. I've brought some special shampoo she might like to try, it's very good, and I've got scissors and a comb. But if she wants her hair washed, I might need to borrow something to dry it with, because I'm thinking of blow-drying it.

Man: Oh … I'm afraid we haven't got a hairdryer, but I can give you a towel if you want.

5 1 Places of interest

2 Listening 💿 1.17–18 **(page 31)**

1

An interesting place to visit while you're staying in England is Woburn Safari Park. This is a place where you can see exciting wild animals from all over the world, but it's not a zoo because the animals do not live in cages. The animals are actually living in a large piece of English countryside, only an hour away from the centre of London, and about the same distance from the country's second city, Birmingham.

Woburn Safari Park is a great place to go for a day out because you can see lots of exciting animals as you drive round the park. And you're not taken round in a coach, you can actually take your own car around a special route that takes you to the parts of the park where the animals live.

And there are animals there from all over the world, including lions and tigers, four completely different sorts of monkey and things like giraffes and elephants too.

There are some rules, of course, both for your own safety and to protect the animals. You can't walk around the park, for instance, and you have to keep your doors and windows closed at all times. Oh, and you're not permitted to eat picnics in the area where the animals live.

So if you're interested in visiting the park, it opens at Easter each year, usually around the beginning of April and you can visit until the 30th October. August is the busiest time, of course, and you might see more people than animals if you go then, but May or September are good months to visit the park.

And when you've completed your tour of the Safari Park, there are other things to do at Woburn. For young people, there is a children's playground and an education centre which has information about the animals. And everyone will enjoy visiting the gift shop where you can buy all sorts of interesting souvenirs of your visit.

2

Now there are lots of things to see and do in the university city of Oxford, especially the old college buildings and the walks along the river. But if you've done all that, and you're looking for a new experience, why not try Oxford Castle?

There's been a castle there for about one thousand years, although the buildings you see today are not as old as that, they're mostly around three hundred years old. In fact, for many years, the present castle buildings were not used as a castle at all. This is because what was called Oxford Castle was actually used as the city's prison. The castle is right in the centre of Oxford, which attracts many tourists from all over the world each year and now the old castle buildings have found a new use.

The buildings are now modernized and most of them are now part of a large hotel. There are 94 bedrooms and a good restaurant, but this is not the main attraction for tourists at the castle. Most of them will want to visit the museum which is in one of the oldest buildings and there is also an art gallery where you can see work by local artists.

In the summer, there is also a lot to do outdoors at the castle. During the day, there is a craft market where you can buy lots of local products, and in the evening there is an open-air theatre. There are also some very nice cafés and shops in the streets near the castle, which you'll enjoy looking round after your visit.

So if you'd like more information about Oxford Castle, this is the number to ring: 0871 873 1256 or log on to the website www.oxfordcastle.com.

6 1 What a bargain!

5 Listening 💿 1.19 **(page 38)**

This is Radio London Fun calling all tourists in London! Did you know that East London has some of the most interesting street markets in Europe?

First up, there's Columbia Road market. You can buy flowers here at any one of 50 stalls. And whatever flowers you choose, they won't cost you much!

Next, there's Brick Lane market. Not everything here is new, but there's something for everybody. And if you're looking for a really good souvenir of London, then check out this market's speciality, leather jackets. You'll have to try one on!

Then, there's Petticoat Lane Market, the oldest and most famous of all London's markets. Buy anything here, from fashionable clothes to toys for the children. Come any morning from Monday to Friday, or on Sunday, when the market is at its biggest and most crowded.

Finally, there's Whitechapel market. It's easy to get to because it's right by the underground station, and just across the road from a hospital. This is the place to buy exotic vegetables and spices from Asia.

So, get down to East London now and be part of the fun!

7 1 Food and drink

2 **Speaking** 🔄 1.20–21 **(page 43)**

3

Examiner:	Your photographs showed people eating a meal. Now I'd like you to talk together about the type of food you eat when you go out and when you stay at home.

4

Examiner:	Your photographs showed people eating a meal. Now I'd like you to talk together about the type of food you eat when you go out and when you stay at home.
Girl:	So, Tom, do you often eat out?
Tom:	Sometimes … sometimes I go out for a meal with my family, and sometimes I go with my friends. What about you?
Girl:	Yes, me too. What type of restaurant does your family go to?
Tom:	Different types, but usually traditional ones. They like to have steak and chips and things like that, but I prefer Italian food …
Girl:	Really! So do I. It's much more interesting than English food, isn't it?
Tom:	Yes, I agree with you about that, and another thing is that it isn't very expensive.
Girl:	That's right. When I go out with my friends, I always go to either an Italian or a Chinese restaurant.
Tom:	Yes, me too … and also Thai … have you tried Thai food?
Girl:	No, what's it like?
Tom:	Well, it's similar to Chinese, but it has different tastes and unusual vegetables.
Girl:	Oh, that sounds good!
Tom:	Yes, you should try it.

3 **Vocabulary** 🔄 1.22–23 **(page 44)**

1

I'm going to tell you how to make tomato owls. First of all, you need some different-sized tomatoes, some big ones and some smaller ones, and a small tin of tuna fish. As well as these two main ingredients, you also need two spoonfuls of mayonnaise, a hard-boiled egg, and some black olives. To give colour, you will also need two spoonfuls of tomato sauce.

You don't have to cook the owls, but to make them you do need some basic equipment. Firstly, you need a mixing bowl to make the mixture in. To make the mixture you need a fork and a spoon, and to cut up the tomatoes and olives you need a fairly sharp knife.

2

So, now I'm going to tell you how to make the tomato owls. Firstly, take the knife and cut the tomatoes in half. Then take the spoon and use it to take the seeds out of the middle of the tomatoes, so that there's a hole for the mixture to go in. Then put the tuna and the hard-boiled egg into the mixing bowl. Then, using a fork, mix them together. When you have a good mixture, stir in the mayonnaise and the tomato sauce, using a spoon. Now take some of the mixture on the spoon and put it into the bottom half of each tomato. Cut the remaining tomato pieces into triangles to make the owl's mouth and ears, and cut up an olive to make its eyes.

7 2 Your own space

3 Listening 1.24 (page 46)

2

Bob: Hello, Mary, how are you?

Mary: Oh, hello Bob. Not too bad. We're having one or two problems with our son Matthew.

Bob: Really? What sort of problems?

Mary: Well, he wants to have his own bedroom, but we haven't got the space and he doesn't seem to understand.

Bob: Oh, so he shares with his brother, does he?

Mary: Yes, but there's not a great age difference, just one year, so you'd think they'd be able to get on together, wouldn't you?

Bob: I remember I used to hate sharing a bedroom with my older brother. We used to argue all the time. Mostly about privacy, as I remember.

Mary: Privacy? You mean you wanted more time to be alone?

Bob: It wasn't that. It was more that I wanted to have my own space. You know, we had one wardrobe, one chest of drawers. I didn't even have one drawer that was all mine, and so my elder brother used to just take all my things if he fancied them.

Mary: Oh, I see. I wonder if that's Matthew's problem? Because he wanted his own computer, but there's not room for two in the one small bedroom, so we said no, they'd have to share.

Bob: So who gets to use it all the time?

Mary: I don't know, but they always seem to be fighting about something, and of course Matthew doesn't have as much homework as his brother, so maybe he doesn't need it so much.

Bob: Well, they're not only for doing homework on, you know.

Mary: I know that Bob, and they've got their own television in the room, but Matthew doesn't really seem to like television very much. I don't understand him sometimes.

Bob: Well, maybe it's because he doesn't get to watch the programmes he likes.

Mary: Actually, I think he'd rather not have the television in the room. I think I'd better talk to them about these things. Maybe we can arrange things better. Thanks, Bob.

Bob: Don't mention it.

5 Listening 1.25 (page 47)

Alice: Oh, hello Harry, how are you?

Harry: Fine, thanks. But you look a bit miserable. What's the matter?

Alice: I've been arguing with my mum again, I'm afraid. I feel sorry about it afterwards, but she just annoys me *so much*.

Harry: Yeah, I know what you mean. But what have you been arguing about?

Alice: Oh, the usual thing about my bedroom.

Harry: Your bedroom?

Alice: Yeah. She's always telling me to tidy it up, but it's my room, so I don't see why I should have to.

Harry: And is it really untidy, or is it just that she's *really* fussy about things like that?

Alice: Oh, it's untidy all right. I mean, you know, I take my clothes off at night and just leave them where they fall.

Harry: And you expect your mum to tidy up after you?

Alice: No. I do it sooner or later because it's not good for your stuff to be left screwed up in a ball, is it? It's just that she wants it done like *now*, and I'm happy to leave it for a while and do it later, you know, when I feel like it, or when I've got friends coming round.

Harry: And so you argue?

Alice: Yeah. She wants me to put everything back in the wardrobe, but I've got so much stuff that it won't all fit anyway.

Harry: You're lucky. I have to share a wardrobe with my brother. He's always wearing my things without asking me.

Alice: But don't you each have your own bedroom?

Harry: We do, but his is very small and you can't get a wardrobe in, so he's always coming in and out of my room to get stuff out of it.

Alice: Oh, I wouldn't like that.

Harry: Nor do I. It leads to *lots* of arguments.

8 1 Close to nature

2 Listening 🔊 1.26 **(page 48)**

1

1

I listened to the weather forecast before we set out and it wasn't encouraging – storms with thunder and lightning and even snow on the hills! Actually, it was a fine, clear day. There was frost on the ground when I woke up and some mist over the fields, but that soon disappeared in the warm sunshine. There were some clouds about, but the wind kept them moving and it didn't rain. All in all, it was a brilliant day!

2

It was lucky we didn't have far to walk on Saturday. I couldn't help slipping on the snow-covered pavements and the air was freezing! But, really, I like that kind of weather best. It kind of makes me feel alive – not like foggy days, or dull, damp ones when I just want to stay indoors, or very hot and sunny ones which send me to sleep! So it was a great day!

3

You know what they say about the weather being changeable? Well, it wasn't like that on Saturday! It was one heavy shower after another – just when we thought it was going to dry up, it started pouring again! Still, it was quite warm, though it got cooler in the evening, so we didn't really mind. I heard later there were gales on the coast, so we escaped them! In spite of the weather, we really enjoyed our day!

5 Listening 🔊 1.27 **(page 50)**

Interviewer:	In the studio today, I have Henry Tweedy and his dog, Lady. Henry, Lady is very special to you, isn't she?
Henry:	Oh yes. We've only been together for six months but I couldn't do without her. I started going deaf when I was twenty and now I can't hear much at all. I can only understand you if I can see your mouth. Lady lets me know when the door bell rings, or my son cries, or about any important noise, at home or when we're out for walks. Guide dogs for the blind are common, but now dogs are regularly trained to help other kinds of disabled people.
Interviewer:	Can any dog be trained like Lady?
Henry:	Many can, and some disabled people ask to have their family pet trained. It helps if the dog is young, but even older dogs like Lady here can learn to do quite difficult things. Her trainer says he knew she was right for the job when he saw how clever she was and how well she got on with people. I'm glad he picked her for me.
Interviewer:	What happened during her training?
Henry:	Well, she spent four months at the training centre, learning to follow instructions and to recognize different sounds. Then the trainer worked with her for two months in my house so she could learn about me and where I live – so that was a six-month training period. The trainer still visits to check everything's going well but we haven't had any problems.
Interviewer:	So, say Lady hears the doorbell, how does she let you know?
Henry:	Well, first she usually runs towards the sound to check it out and then she comes back to tell me about it. She does that by pushing her nose into some part of my body. For the doorbell, it's my left knee.
Interviewer:	And how do you tell her what to do?
Henry:	She's always looking at me, ready for any command, and I talk to her with my hands – it's a kind of sign language. I sometimes reward her afterwards with a biscuit, but not all the time because it's bad for her.
Interviewer:	Do you think Lady enjoys her work?
Henry:	Oh, without a doubt! Dogs like having a job to do – they have quite a professional attitude to it! Lady is happiest when she's busy or learning to do something new. Many family dogs sleep most of the day but that's not really natural for them.
Interviewer:	Well, thank you Henry, and Lady. It's been fascinating talking to you.

10 1 Entertainment

3 Listening 🔘 1.28–30 **(page 61)**

1

Man: What do you feel like doing tonight? I'm getting a bit tired of clubbing.

Woman: Yeah, me too. How about going to the open-air concert? The guitarist is meant to be *really* good.

Man: Oh, I heard that all the tickets were sold out weeks ago, but there's a good film on at the ABC. You know, it's the one that won all the Oscars.

Woman: OK, and if we can't get in, there's always the theatre next door. That's never full, so it's a good idea.

2

Woman: It's *great*, this new cinema! *Four* films on at the same time, and they're all good.

Man: Well, I don't know about that. There's a good thriller on in Screen Number One, or I wouldn't mind seeing the science fiction one, that's meant to be really good.

Woman: Well, I'm not keen on seeing either of those. But how about the one about animals, that's much more my sort of thing than the other one ... what is it? Some sort of romantic comedy?

Man: That's right. Oh well, I'm quite happy to go along with your choice.

3

Man: So, what did you think of it?

Woman: Well, he's a brilliant director, isn't he? All those lovely scenes in the mountains ... the camerawork was *wonderful*.

Man: I thought the actors were good on the whole, although to be honest, I think the storyline, the plot, is *so* strong that you don't worry so much about the characters. I mean, it is a classic action film, isn't it?

Woman: I *absolutely* agree with you. I was on the edge of my seat the whole time! You never knew what was going to happen next. That's what *really* made it for me.

Man: Oh yeah, me too.

5 Listening 🔘 1.31 **(page 62)**

It's now five to eight and there's just time for one more song before the news, but before I do that, I'd just like to tell you about one or two things coming up later today on your local radio station.

First of all, after the eight o'clock news, at 8.15, we have our *Arts Review* programme. Debbie Clarke will be telling you about what's on in the region in the coming week, including information about theatre, cinema and concerts. Today Debbie will also have a special guest in the studio, Kevin Jones, who is the drummer with the very successful pop band, *Splodge*. Kevin will be talking about what it's like to be the drummer rather than the lead singer in a pop band.

That's followed at 8.45 by the weather forecast. Graham Smith will be here to tell you if it's going to be wet or fine for the rest of the week. Let's hope that Graham has some good news for us. After that, at 8.50, a new series begins. Polly Brown has been out and about in the countryside this week talking to people who are interested in wild flowers. And I must say that some of those people really know a great deal about the subject.

After that, at 9.30, we have *The Cookery Programme*. James Grant will be back with some more delicious recipes, and he'll also be telling us what to look out for when we're buying fresh fruit and vegetables. And finally, at 10.15, we have this morning's radio play. *Happy Times* it's called, and it tells the story of two children's summer holiday by the seaside and something which happened that was to change their lives forever. Sounds good. So, that's it on your favourite station today. Now up to the news here is *Splodge* with their latest single, which is called *'Take me'*.

Recording scripts for Practice Test 1

Practice Test 1 – Paper 2 Listening

Page 72   PART 1

RUBRIC = R

R   There are seven questions in this part. For each question there are three pictures and a short recording. Choose the correct picture and put a tick in the box below it.

Before we start, here is an example.

R   Where did the man leave his sunglasses?

M   Oh no! I've lost my sunglasses.
F   Well, you had them on in the car. Perhaps you left them inside?
M   No, I remember taking them off when we parked outside the restaurant. Perhaps I left them in there, or in that shop we went into, just before we had lunch.
F   No, you didn't leave them in the shop, because you put them on the table while we were eating. They must still be there. Come on. We'll go and get them.

R   The second picture is correct so there is a tick in box B.

Look at the three pictures for question one now.

R   Now we are ready to start. Listen carefully.

You will hear each recording twice.

R   One. What will the woman buy?

F   Do you need anything at the shops? I've got to go down to the chemist's because I need a new toothbrush.
M   Well, two things really – some toothpaste and some shampoo. They've both nearly run out.
F   I bought you some toothpaste yesterday. It's in a bag on the chair in the bathroom. I saw that it was nearly finished and there's enough shampoo. See you later, then.
M   Bye.

R   Two. Where is the woman's cookery book?

F   Have you seen my new cookery book?
M   I think I last saw it out in the garden on the seat under the tree.
F   Well, I was looking at it in the garden, but I've looked, and it's not there now. I brought it inside I think, but it doesn't seem to be on the dining-room table with my other things.
M   Look here it is, on the shelf with all the others. Your sister must have put it back when she came in from the garden.
F   Oh good.

R   Three. What time will the next train for Bristol leave?

M   This is an announcement for passengers travelling to Bristol this morning. Unfortunately, because of bad weather overnight, the 07.45 service to Bristol is cancelled and will not run today. The next direct train to Bristol will be the 08.25 which will depart from platform three. Those passengers for London who plan to change at Bristol should take the 08.05 service to Southampton and change there onto a London train. Tickets via Bristol will be valid on this train this morning.

R   Four. Which yoghurt does the girl choose?

M   Jill, you must be hungry. You've been studying for hours. How about something to eat?
F   Oh thanks, Dad. It is time I had a break. Have we got any of that chocolate ice cream you bought for my birthday?
M   Your brother finished it off this morning, I'm afraid. But we've got some yoghurt. Do you want that? There's banana, strawberry or lemon.
F   Oh I'm not keen on strawberry, so I'd rather have the banana. I do like the lemon but I had one earlier actually.

R   Five. Which band is the girl talking about?

M   Have you found any good music on the Internet lately?
F   Yeah, I found this brilliant new band called the Black Bunnies. They've got their own website and you can download a sample track which is really cool.
M   Oh, I think I saw them on the television. Is that the band with the girl on the drums?
F   Well, there wasn't a drummer on the clip I saw,

just two boys on guitar and a girl with an electric violin – one of the boys is also the lead singer.

M Oh right.

R **Six. What did the boy get for his birthday?**

F Hey, I like the new swimming shorts! Were they a birthday present?

M Oh thanks. Actually I bought these myself when I was at the beach last weekend. I asked for money for my birthday, so that I could buy myself a surfboard – but unfortunately my mum decided to get me these trainers instead.

F Well, they're very nice, even if they're not exactly what you wanted.

R **Seven. Which animal will be on the television programme first?**

F And in tonight's edition of *Animal Tales* we're going to see stories about both wild and pet animals, plus some who are not quite sure if they're wild or not. Like the parrot that escaped from its cage and lived for a week in a city park and the frog that decided to make its home in twelve-year-old Samantha James's bedroom. But before that, we're off to hear the story of Max, a six-month-old puppy who, rather like our escaped parrot, got a taste of freedom this week.

R **That is the end of Part 1.**

Page 73   PART 2

R **Now turn to Part 2, questions 8–13.**

You will hear an interview with a woman who has written a popular novel.

For each question, put a tick in the correct box. You now have 45 seconds to look at the questions for Part 2.

Now we are ready to start. Listen carefully. You will hear the recording twice.

I Today I'm talking to the writer, Anna Zayuna. Anna, did you always want to write?

AZ I wrote my first novel when I was thirteen. It was based on the life of a teacher. I even sent it to a publisher, but they weren't interested. When I got to college, I didn't think I could make a living as a writer. So I trained as a nurse because I wanted to help people, and forgot about writing.

I What happened to change that?

AZ Well, I met my husband when I was 20. I'd graduated and had my wedding within a few months of each other at the age of 22 and had the first of three children at 24, so my career was fairly interrupted. Later, when the children grew up a bit, I did a writing class as a hobby, and then got some work as a journalist as a result.

I How were you discovered?

AZ I wrote a short story and entered it for a competition on the Internet. I won second place and my story was published in a magazine. Then I was asked to read the story on the radio. An agent heard that, and asked me to develop the story into a novel. It took me three years, and things just took off from there.

I Is the novel about you?

AZ I grew up in a small town which is actually the one that Sally – the little girl in the book – describes. But our families couldn't be more different. My father still runs his insurance firm and my mother's a full-time housewife. It was a lovely home life, and I definitely wasn't as brave as Sally is.

I The book's about Sally and her horse. Do you like horses?

AZ I've always liked them, but I'd never owned one. But when I started writing the book, I realized what a big part of the story they were going to become. It was fun visiting a stables to see how you look after them properly. It's not really the kind of work I'd like to do though.

I What advice would you give young writers?

AZ Oh I'd say, don't wait for the perfect time to start writing, but find some spare moments every day to do just a little. Also, don't sit down and expect this beautiful stream of words to flow – you have to be patient. I had to keep going back and changing things in my book until they were right. But don't give up, because it's worth it in the end.

I Anna. Thank you.

R **That is the end of Part 2.**

Page 73   PART 3

R **Now turn to Part 3, questions 14–19.**

You will hear a student giving a talk about a person she admires.

For each question, fill in the missing information in the numbered space.

You now have 20 seconds to look at Part 3.

Now we are ready to start. Listen carefully. You will hear the recording twice.

F   The person I've chosen to talk about is a spaceman – whose job involves travelling in outer space. His name is Michael Foale and, although he now works mostly in the USA, he was actually born in England, and has also spent time working on the Russian Mir space-station.

Michael's taken part in four space-shuttle missions and holds the US record for spending the most time in space – that's 374 days in total – including one period of four and a half months in a space-station.

As a boy, Michael was very keen on both science and flying, and chose to study physics at university. His first job after leaving university was with a company that built aeroplanes in the USA. After that, in 1987, he got a job with NASA, the US space agency and his first space flight was in 1992.

In 1999, Michael made his first space walk and has now spent more than twenty-two hours walking in space. He is often given jobs to do during his space walks, which can be quite difficult wearing a spacesuit and gloves.

One of Michael's space walks included the most difficult thing that he has ever had to do in space. He had the job of putting a new computer in a satellite as it went around the Earth. If he'd done anything wrong, the satellite would have stopped working. The job took him 45 minutes and afterwards everything worked perfectly.

Michael says that one of the most surprising things about travelling in space is the wonderful colours you see. He says there are lots of different greens, blues and reds. And the Moon appears to be brown – which he says was the biggest surprise of all as he'd always thought of it as yellow.

Michael Foale is someone I truly admire. Thank you.

R   **That is the end of Part 3.**

Page 74   PART 4

R   **Now turn to Part 4, questions 20–25.**

Look at the six sentences for this part. You will hear a conversation between a girl, Tanya, and a boy, Marek, about their holiday plans.

Decide if each sentence is correct or incorrect. If it is correct, put a tick in the box under A for YES. If it is not correct, put a tick in the box under B for NO.

You now have 20 seconds to look at the questions for Part 4.

Now we are ready to start. Listen carefully. You will hear the recording twice.

T   Hi, Marek. Are you looking forward to your holidays?

M   Oh Tanya, I can't wait!

T   Where is it you're going? Is it camping on an island somewhere or am I thinking of someone else?

M   Well, we were going camping, but my Dad's just bought a camper van, so we're going in that instead. It means you can go to other countries without having to get a flight which is good in a way, but actually I always used to enjoy sleeping in a tent.

T   Yeah, I know what you mean, but it must be nice getting to see all the scenery along the way. I have to say the flight is my least favourite part of going abroad on holiday.

M   Oh I never mind it actually – and the airport can be quite fun sometimes.

T   You must be joking! All those people and nothing to do except look round expensive shops. I mean, you always end up buying something you don't really want, just because there's nothing else to do.

M   Oh, I don't. Anyway, where are you off to this year? Florida again?

T   Well, I'm getting a bit old for Disneyland, Marek, though my little brother would still like it. We're actually going somewhere new. It's like a sports camp where you stay with lots of other kids and learn how to do different activities.

M   You mean you're going without your parents?

T   Not exactly. I mean they're there too doing whatever they want – golf in my dad's case – but you only actually see them at mealtimes.

M   Sounds cool. But will you have to look after your little brother?

T   No way. They divide you up according to age. He'll be doing football and swimming and all that, whereas I get to go water skiing.

M   Wow! Doesn't that cost a fortune?

T   Well, quite a bit so I'm just doing it on one of the days. But there's windsurfing and water polo too.

M   I see.

R   **That is the end of Part 4.**

You now have six minutes to check and copy your answers onto the answer sheet.

You have one more minute.

That is the end of the test.

Notes on the model Speaking test

Practice Test 1 – Paper 3 Speaking

pages 74–76

On the course CD, a model Speaking test has been recorded. It comes between Practice Test 1 and Practice Test 2, which are both Listening tests. In the recording of the Speaking test, actors play the part of students. They perform the test tasks using PET-level language, but without mistakes of grammar, vocabulary or pronunciation.

Students should use the model Speaking test to help them understand the best way to do the tasks. Remember, the examination tests the ability to speak spontaneously and to interact with another person. This means that it is not possible to learn what to say in advance. It is, however, a good idea to practise and be ready to perform the tasks in the best way.

In the recording, each part of the Speaking test is played separately. Students are using the materials in Practice Test 1, Speaking on pages 74–76. Students preparing for the PET Speaking test should listen to each part, think about how the students do each task, and then attempt the same tasks themselves. They should not try to remember actual words, as they will need to give their own opinions and ideas. This will, however, be easier for them once they have heard a model.

For each task, a list of things to listen for is included below. Students can either work individually, or in pairs as a classroom activity. Students may need to listen to each part more than once. They should look at the visual materials on pages 75–76 as they listen to Parts 2 and 3.

PART 1

In Part 1, students should answer the examiner's questions. (See page 7 for more information.)

Listen and notice:
- how many questions each student is asked
- how long their answers are
- the types of question each student is asked
- how the students make what they say interesting.

Notice also:
- when the students are asked to spell their names.

PART 2

In Part 2, students talk about the situation in a picture. (See pages 13 and 75 for more information.)

Listen and notice:
- how many times the instructions are given
- how the students begin
- how long each student speaks for
- how each student shows interest in what the other is saying
- how many of the pictures they talk about
- when they reach a decision.

PART 3

In Part 3, each student talks about a photograph. (See pages 40 and 76 for more information.)

Listen and notice:
- the topic of the photographs
- how each student begins
- the type of things they talk about
- what they do if they don't know a word.

PART 4

In Part 4, the students have a discussion on the same topic as Part 3, but giving their own opinions. (See page 43 for more information.)

Listen and notice:
- the two things the students are asked to talk about
- how they begin
- how long each student speaks
- how each student shows interest in what the other is saying
- how they agree and disagree.

> **Note:** the Speaking tests in Ready for PET are sample tests only. They are not actual Cambridge ESOL past papers.

Recording scripts for Practice Test 2

Practice Test 2 – Paper 2 Listening

Page 83   PART 1

RUBRIC = R

R   There are seven questions in this part. For each question there are three pictures and a short recording. Choose the correct picture and put a tick in the box below it.

Before we start, here is an example.

R   Where did the man leave his sunglasses?

M   Oh no! I've lost my sunglasses.
F   Well, you had them on in the car. Perhaps you left them inside?
M   No, I remember taking them off when we parked outside the restaurant. Perhaps I left them in there, or in that shop we went into, just before we had lunch.
F   No, you didn't leave them in the shop, because you put them on the table while we were eating. They must still be there. Come on. We'll go and get them.

R   The second picture is correct so there is a tick in box B.

Look at the three pictures for question one now.

R   Now we are ready to start. Listen carefully.

You will hear each recording twice.

R   One. Where will they go on holiday?

F   We'd better start thinking about where to go on holiday this year. If we wait too long, everything at the seaside will be booked up.
M   I'd like to do something really different this year. My boss was saying he and his wife went to stay on a farm, and they helped to look after the animals and pick the fruit. It would make a change from lying on the beach or walking in the mountains.
F   What a good idea! Let's do that. Can you ask him for the details?
M   Yes, OK.

R   Two. What are they cleaning?

F   Well, it's going to be a long job cleaning this. It's dirtier than I thought!
M   Don't worry, we've got all afternoon. Have you got two sponges and some shampoo? I'll start at the front, and you start at the back.
F   No, I want to do the wheels first. Shall we clean inside too? The seats look really dirty, and there's rubbish all over the floor.
M   Well, I told Dad that we'd wash it. If we're going to do the inside too, we need to ask for more money.
F   Good idea.

R   Three: Where is the water coming from?

M   Look, there's water all over the floor! Last time this happened you hadn't shut the fridge properly and all the ice melted.
F   Well, it's not open now. It must be that big plant in the corner. You've given it too much water as usual.
M   I haven't watered it for days, actually. And in any case, the water seems to be on the other side of it. The washing machine's been making a funny noise again lately, and the plant's next to that.
F   Yes, you're right. Look there's water all round it.

R   Four. What will they eat at the picnic?

F   What shall we take to eat at the picnic? I've got some chicken legs in the fridge.
M   Oh, not again! We always have those when we go on a picnic. Let's take the same as when we went to Scotland last year. It was delicious.
F   What, you mean the cheese sandwiches?
M   Actually, I was thinking of that pasta salad with olives and tomatoes. We could take some paper plates to eat it off. The sandwiches are what we had when we went to Wales. I don't want those again.
F   OK.

R   Five. What subject will the class do first this morning?

F   OK, now listen. There's a slight change to the timetable this morning because Marie, the French assistant, is off sick. You'll still be having computer studies and art as usual today, but it will be art instead of French after the morning break and computer studies up until the break. We hope that Serge, the other French assistant, will be able to give you your conversation class this afternoon, instead of this morning. But he's not here this morning, so we'll have to wait and see.

R Six. Which T-shirt does the girl choose?

M Come on Julia, hurry up and decide which T-shirt you want. I can't stand here all day!

F Well, I like this one with lions on it, but the one with the dolphins is nice too.

M What about this one with bears? Look, they're really cute.

F Dad I'm not wearing a T-shirt with teddy-bears on it! How old do you think I am? OK, I'll have the dolphins, because the lions don't look very real anyway.

M Right.

R Seven. Which suitcase does the woman buy?

F Excuse me, I'd like to buy a suitcase, please. Can you tell me the difference between these three here?

M Well, the real leather one is the most expensive but is very good quality. The plastic one is the cheapest, but if you want my opinion, I'd buy a metal one.

F I see. That's the mid-priced one.

M It is. Everybody's using them because, although they're not the cheapest, they're almost unbreakable and quite light to carry.

F OK, I'll take it.

R That is the end of Part 1.

Page 84   PART 2

R Now turn to Part 2, questions 8–13.

You will hear an interview with Stella Brady who is a professional photographer.

For each question, put a tick in the correct box. You now have 45 seconds to look at the questions for Part 2.

Now we are ready to start. Listen carefully. You will hear the recording twice.

I Stella, you're a professional photographer, when did you start?

SB Well, I entered my first photographic competition at the age of ten. I'd started taking photographs when I got my first camera at the age of eight. I didn't win that first competition, I had to wait until I was twelve for that – but I was the youngest

competitor and the judge said how good I was for my age – it was great.

I So how did you learn?

SB Well, my parents bought me the camera – but they didn't know much about it. It was actually my uncle, David, who taught my brother and me. He took photographs for a local newspaper and when we were little, he used to take us along with him to see famous people, that sort of thing. My brother wasn't that interested, but for some reason I was.

I And did you go into this job straight from school?

SB No, you see, my uncle went to live in Australia when I was twelve. I missed him, but I didn't stop taking photographs and my big dream in life was to go and visit him out there. But I couldn't afford a holiday – I needed to save up some money. So I trained as an electrician and did that for two years.

I Then you went to Australia?

SB That's right. I visited my uncle, then travelled round taking photographs. I did get work with newspapers out there, but mostly I was selling photos of famous sights to tourists – that sort of thing. I realized that, although I'd learnt a lot – I'd find it difficult to make a living as a photographer out there – so I came home.

I And now you've got your own photographic studio?

SB Yes, in my home town. I began with sports photography because I like football – but I soon realized that you made more money doing wedding photos. But those are not the photos I put up in my studio. I do some artistic work – photos of landscapes and things – it's more a hobby than anything else, but the studio's full of them.

I So what are your plans for the future?

SB Well, I'm thinking of developing my skills as a portrait photographer – you know – close-up photos of people that look a bit like oil paintings. It's quite hard to do actually because you want people to look natural and the light has to be right. You usually have to take hundreds of shots before you get the perfect one. But it's worth it.

R That is the end of Part 2.

Page 84   PART 3

R Now turn to Part 3, questions 14–19.

You will hear a tour guide talking to some visitors in a jewellery workshop.

For each question, fill in the missing information in the numbered space.

You now have 20 seconds to look at Part 3.

Now we are ready to start. Listen carefully. You will hear the recording twice.

M   Good morning. I'd like to welcome you to our jewellery workshop. Before we begin our tour, where you'll have the chance to meet some of our artists, let me tell you a little about the history of the workshop.

It was started five years ago by a group of artists from different countries who had studied here in London. Although there are also artists from Asia and South America in the group, it is artists from Africa who really lead the workshop, and the style of the pieces of jewellery made here reflects that.

You will see people making jewellery made out of many different materials. Gold is the metal that we use most of all, but you will also see both copper and silver as well. Also, don't expect to see too many expensive stones like diamonds. We do use them, but you are more likely to see shells and even sometimes seeds used instead.

When an artist makes a piece of jewellery, they usually begin with a shape, and you'll see them working from drawings as we walk around. Then they have to select a colour and a material. Many of the artists here get their ideas from music, so you'll hear some of that as we walk around too. Even so, artists often make many trial pieces before they get the design just right.

Although we do make rings, necklaces and earrings like all jewellers, this workshop is most famous for jewellery that can be worn in the hair. If you'd like to try on any of the pieces, there will be a chance to do this in the gallery and shop which we'll visit at the end of the tour.

So, if you're all ready, I'll take you …

R   That is the end of Part 3.

Page 85   PART 4

R   Now turn to Part 4, questions 20–25.

Look at the six sentences for this part. You will hear a conversation between a boy, Darren, and a girl, Monica, about a football match.

Decide if each sentence is correct or incorrect. If it is correct, put a tick in the box under A for YES. If it is not correct, put a tick in the box under B for NO.

You now have 20 seconds to look at the questions for Part 4.

Now we are ready to start. Listen carefully. You will hear the recording twice.

F   I saw you at the football match, Darren. Did you have a good time?
M   Really? I didn't know you were there, Monica. Why didn't you come over and say hello?
F   Well, I saw you in the distance, but then I lost sight of you in the crowd. There were a lot of people there, weren't there?
M   Well, it was a normal sort of crowd for a home game.
F   Oh right. I have been before, but not for a couple of years. Some friends of mine are over from Italy and they wanted to see a match – so I took them.
M   And what did they think of the new stadium?
F   Well I think they're used to big stadiums like that in Italy, so they weren't that impressed – but I thought it was a great improvement on the old one.
M   Oh, a lot better. I don't know whether it's worth the amount they ask for a ticket though – that's certainly gone up a lot.
F   Has it? I thought it compared quite well with the cost of any other afternoon out – you know, about the same as a concert or going to the theatre.
M   If you go every week, it mounts up though. Anyway, did you enjoy the match?
F   It was alright. But my friends reckon that football's more exciting in Italy and I think they may be right – you know, more stylish.
M   What do you mean? Our local team's very stylish and we've got two Italian players in the squad anyway.
F   I'd like to have seen a few goals though. I mean a goalless draw is not exactly what you hope to see, is it?
M   I thought the team did really well actually – they were just unfortunate not to hit the back of the net – they had plenty of chances.
F   OK, if you insist.

R   That is the end of Part 4.

You now have six minutes to check and copy your answers onto the answer sheet.

You have one more minute.

That is the end of the test.

Examples of student writing

In PET Writing Part 2, students are required to write a short communicative message, and in PET Writing Part 3 they have to write either an informal letter or a story. (For more details refer to pages 10, 37 and 38.)

A maximum of 5 marks is available in PET Writing Part 2. In this part, the focus of assessment is on successful communication of the message. Students will score high marks if they have conveyed the three points in the instructions clearly.

In PET Writing Part 3, 15 marks are available. The focus of assessment in this part is the student's ability to organize ideas clearly and to convey them using a range of language. Assessment is based on the correct use of spelling and punctuation; on accurate and appropriate use of a variety of grammatical structures; and on the use of topic-related vocabulary and linking words.

At this level, students are not expected to produce writing which is completely free from errors. A mistake that does not prevent the writer from being understood is considered less serious than a mistake that interferes with communication. Students are given credit for being ambitious in attempting a range of different structures, even if they make some errors.

The following examples were written by students attempting the Practice Tests on pages 70–71 and 81–82. The examiner's comment 'adequate attempt' indicates the minimum standard of writing necessary to achieve a pass at PET level.

Practice Test 1, Writing Part 2

1

> Hello Sam,
> I'm really sorry, I can't come your birthday party. My mother will be operated next week so I should go there to look after her. A friend of me his name is Andy can take the photos. His mobile phone is 07777665522.
> Happy birthday!
> Nuria

Examiner's comment: 5 marks
The three points in the instructions for this task are included and expressed clearly. The minor language errors ('*come your birthday party*', '*My mother will be operated*', '*A friend of me his name is Andy*') don't prevent the message from being understood.

2

> To Sam
> Your 18th birthday party is next week. I'm sorry I can't go to the party. I am going play football match in another city and I going back too late. I'm very sorry. I think is good party.
> Martin

Examiner's comment: 3 marks
One of the points from the instructions for this task ('*suggest someone else who can take the photos*') has been left out, so this student can't score more than 3 marks. However, the other two points are expressed clearly in spite of some language errors ('*going play football*', '*I going back*', '*I think is good party*').

Practice Test 1, Writing Part 3 (letter)

3

> Dear Victoria:
> I am pleased to get your letter.
> Which school has not good and bad things? I think every one has both of them, whether is there rich people or poor people. The best of my school is having professional teachers, they are people who have given their complete life to teach and they know do it in the best way. Another good thing is because is a responsable institution, they give you all classes on time and use the appropriate material to teach easier.
> One of the bad things is my school is long way my house and so I am travelling two hours in the train every day.
> In conclusion, I say to you "Good school depend of good student."
> Please write to me again soon.
> Your friend,
> Marisa

Examiner's comment: very good attempt
This student writes confidently and is ambitious in her use of language. She produces a variety of present tenses, usually appropriately, and attempts some complex sentence patterns with '*whether*', '*who*' and '*because*'. She shows good control of school-related vocabulary ('*professional teachers*', '*responsable institution*', '*classes*', '*appropriate material*'). Ideas are clearly organized in paragraphs and some simple linking devices are used ('*Another good thing*', '*One of the bad things*', '*and so*', '*In conclusion*'). The letter begins and ends in an appropriate way. There are a few minor errors ('*whether is there*', '*they know do it*', '*responsable*', '*to teach easier*', '*long way my house*', '*depend of*') but they are made because the student is being ambitious in her use of language and they do not prevent communication of the ideas.

4

> Dear penfriend,
> Thank you for your letter. I can tell you about my school. My school is beautiful and big, and it has a good organization. The subjects are very interesting and easy. But I have a lot to study. My school has a lot of classrooms, two shops to buy sweets and a very long stairs. In my classroom there is a TV, a video recorder, a new DVD and many computers. I love all of this in my school.
>   But I hate my school when the teachers give me a lot of homework, when I can't say my ideas and when the teachers give me a surprise test.
> Bruno

Examiner's comment: adequate attempt

This student's letter has few language errors but it is very unambitious in its use of language and lacks variety. The present simple tense is the only tense used and the only complex sentence pattern attempted is with 'when'. The student shows control of basic school-related vocabulary ('organization', 'classrooms', 'computers', 'teachers', 'homework', 'surprise test'). There is an attempt to organize the ideas into paragraphs and the linkers 'and' and 'but' are used. There is an appropriate beginning to the letter, and it has a signature at the end although the ending is rather abrupt.

5

> I'm lucky because my school is realy good and usualy I love it. But somtimes I just hate it. My school is in Fernando Pessoa street I go to school Monday Tusday Wedsday Thursday and Friday. I like talk my frends and play footbal. My history techer is good techer I must going the room. This all about my school.

Examiner's comment: poor attempt

It is difficult to make an assessment of this student's work as it is so short. The student has also copied the first two sentences directly from the input text. The language used is very basic, there are many errors and the meaning of the penultimate sentence is unclear. The writer makes no attempt to follow letter-writing conventions and does not address the reader directly, begin or end the letter appropriately or sign it.

Practice Test 1, Writing Part 3 (story)

6

> The message in the sand
> Once upon a time Josh was kidnapped by some pirates. They took Josh to their boat and there an adventure started. The boy decided to escape because he was very scared. Paco, the pirate boss caught Josh and slapped him. The boy started to cry, so Paco pushed him to the sea.
>   Josh was very afraid. Fortunately he saw an island and he swam towards there.
>   He was very hungry and tired so he felt asleep on the sand. When he woke up he looked for a stem to fish. Later, he saw a boat coming so he wrote a message in the sand. The people on the boat never saw the message. Josh is story now.

Examiner's comment: good attempt

This student is ambitious in his use of language. He uses the past simple correctly and appropriately with a variety of regular and irregular verbs, including a passive form. He attempts some complex sentence patterns using 'because' and 'when'. He makes use of a good range of adventure-related vocabulary ('kidnapped', 'pirates', 'escape', 'scared', 'caught', 'slapped', 'pushed'). The narrative develops clearly with ideas organized in paragraphs and linked through connectors ('Once upon a time', 'so', 'Fortunately', 'Later'). Unfortunately, the meaning of the final sentence is not entirely clear, which detracts from the overall impression the story makes. There are few other language errors ('to the sea', 'felt asleep', 'stem') and these do not impede understanding of the story.

7

> This is the story about three boys. They had lived a libely childhood together, during the summers they went near a sea and they had joined to play and spend their time together. Every day they went to the beach and they had used to leaves differents messages in the sand, they invented a new alphabet and they created differents signs that nobody else had untherstood. One day one of the boys was kidnaped, all the city was upset, the people went by differents places but nobody could found the boy. But the friends thought about their old play and went to the beach. There they could found the signs and they translate its to the police. A few hours later the police could find the house where three man had a little boy. They could rescue him without problems because they acted quickly by surprise.

Examiner's comment: adequate attempt

This student attempts to use a range of structures but there are many errors and control of past tenses is weak. There is some good use of vocabulary which is appropriate to the story ('*childhood*', '*spend their time*', '*invented a new alphabet*', '*created differents signs*', '*kidnaped*', '*upset*', '*translate*', '*rescue*'). The narrative progresses smoothly through the use of time phrases ('*during the summers*', '*Every day*', '*One day*', '*A few hours later*') and the connectors '*and*' and '*but*'. The story has a good introductory sentence and an appropriate concluding sentence. The story is not penalised for being a bit long but the extra length means there are more errors. The errors mostly do not impede understanding.

8

> One day I read the message in the sand. The message is JOHN LOVE ROSA so I am Rosa but who is John? I am walking at the beach I am looking at all peoples. Are you John? Are you John? Nobody are speaking. All people are thinking she is mad girl. I want know John. May be he is good man. Then I see my father at the beach, he have small dog. He give dog he say this dog his name is John and he is to you and I think he love you. Now I can understand the message in the sand!

Examiner's comment: inadequate attempt

This is a fairly coherent story but the language used is limited and there are many basic errors, some of which obscure the meaning. Control of verb forms is weak and there is no attempt to use anything other than present tenses. The vocabulary used is also limited. An attempt is made to use narrative markers ('*One day*', '*Then*', '*Now*') but the story is not organized into paragraphs. The story has appropriate beginning and ending sentences.

Practice Test 2, Writing Part 2

9

> Hello,
> My husband and me our flat is 34 to the left of yours. This place is so quiet but sometimes on weekend the family in the 53 like to make parties until midnight. Came you want with us take a delicious English tea.
> Regards, Martha and Jack

Examiner's comment: 4 marks

The three points in the instructions for this task are included and the first two points are expressed clearly in spite of some minor language errors ('*My husband and me our flat*', '*on weekend*', '*make parties*'). However, the third point, the offer, is not very clearly expressed meaning this candidate scores 4 rather than 5 points.

10

> Hello! My name is Noemi. I live here for three years. So I can give you some information about my town. There is a big supermarket at the end of this street. You can buy any kinds of food there.

Examiner's comment: 3 marks

One of the points from the instructions for this task ('*offer to do something for the family*') has been left out, so this student can't score more than 3 marks. However, the other two points are expressed clearly in spite of some language errors ('*I live here for three years*', '*any kinds of food*').

Practice Test 2, Writing Part 3 (letter)

11

> Dear Daniel,
> I'm so glad to receive your letter! And I'm very happy to know you are coming in Italy! In my opinion, you must visit Florence, which is wonderful, and Uffizi with all the history of the Renaissance. Then you can visit Siena, Arezzo and Pisa, with the famous tower and the nature, which is wonderful.
> After enjoying yourself in this way, you can visit Assisi or Gubbio, both are beautiful as Medieval towns, and going sightseeing is like a time-travel.
> We've also got a lot of museums, good restaurants (our cousine is the best of the world) and festivals of every kind you want. Isn't it a fantastic reason to come?
> See you as soon as possible.
> Kisses,
> Valeria.

Examiner's comment: good attempt

This student is fairly ambitious in her use of language and attempts to employ a more than adequate range of structures, including the use of complex sentence patterns with '*which*', '*After*' and '*both*'. She demonstrates a range of vocabulary which is more than adequate for the task ('*history of the Renaissance*', '*famous tower*', '*Medieval towns*', '*going sightseeing*', '*time-travel*', '*fantastic reason*'), though there is repetition of '*wonderful*'. The ideas are organized clearly in paragraphs and there is an attempt to use connecting words and phrases ('*In my opinion*', '*then*', '*After enjoying yourself in this way*'). The letter begins and ends appropriately and will have a positive effect on the reader. There are few errors, none of which impede communication of the ideas.

12

> My dear Rachel,
> I'm very happy you planning to visit Korea. You can find the history everywhere but I very recommend you go to Kyongju. This is beautful place it has a lot old tumbs and casels. You like beautful montans? You can go Sorak-san national park, it very beautful place all time but in autum it very much beautful because trees are going red and gold color. Do not forget our capital city Seoul it has many intersting places for visiters. You like spicy food? You can use the chopsticks? I take you very good restoran in my city Seoul. Come to Korea soon!
> Your friend   Hyung Pun

Examiner's comment: adequate attempt

This student is not ambitious in her use of language but there is an adequate range of structures. There is a fairly good range of vocabulary (*'tumbs'*, *'casels'*, *'montans'*, *'autum'*, *'capital city'*, *'spicy food'*, *'chopsticks'*) but this is marred by spelling errors and repetition of some words (*'beautful'*, *'place'*). The ideas are organized logically but the organization would be improved by the use of paragraphs. The letter has an appropriate beginning and ending. Although there are a number of errors, these do not impede communication.

Practice Test 2, Writing Part 3 (story)

13

> Emma didn't know how to find the money she needed. She wanted to buy a beautiful jacket which she had seen in a shop window. Unfortunately she had already received her pocket money and spent it on a gift. She knew that jacket it was the only one left. So she tried working like a baby-sitter, a waitress, a dog-sitter. Finally, at the end of the mounth, she had collected enought money to buy what she wanted. She run into the shop and looked at the jacket. What a terrible surprice! She realized that she had read the price wrongly. Infact it had one more zero. She felt really sad, tourned back home and ... on her bed there was a big present, and all her friends shouted "Happy Birthday". It was her birthday but she had been so concentrated in work that she hadn't remember it! The present was the jacket! What a careless and lucky girl!

Examiner's comment: good attempt

This student uses fairly ambitious language. She uses both past and past perfect tenses appropriately and mostly accurately, and attempts some complex sentence patterns with *'which'* and *'so ... that'*. There is also a range of vocabulary appropriate to the task (*'pocket money'*, *'spent it on'*, *'baby-sitter'*, *'waitress'*, *'dog-sitter'*, *'read the price wrongly'*, *'concentrated'*). The story develops well and although it is not organized in paragraphs, good use is made of linking words (*'Unfortunately'*, *'So'*, *'finally'*, *'Infact'*). The story comes to an effective resolution and the errors do not impede communication.

14

> Emma didn't know how to find the money she needed. She thinks in diferents forms to collect money. One of the ideas are collect money selling lemonade. Other way for collect money was working in a fast food restaurant six hours a day but she only have one mounth to collect $130 and working in the restaurant she will collect $120. She goes to her best friend house Sue to talk with her. They talk and talk and then Sue say this: Why don't you work in the fast-food restaurant and when you finish working you come to sell lemonade. Emma liked the idea of doing that and she starting do it. At the end of the mounth she collect $150 and Emma could buy the bike she want.

Examiner's comment: adequate attempt

This student's use of language is fairly unambitious. The initial sentence (provided) is in the past tense but there are few past tenses in the rest of the story. Complex sentence patterns are rarely attempted and ideas are mainly connected using *'and'* and *'but'*. There is an adequate range of vocabulary for the task (*'selling lemonade'*, *'fast food restaurant'*) although there is repetition of *'collect'*. The story develops well through the use of appropriate linkers (*'One of the ideas'*, *'Other way'*, *'then'*, *'At the end of the mounth'*) although ideas are not organized into paragraphs. The story comes to a successful resolution and the errors do not impede communication.

Wordlist

Unit 1 Lesson 1
advice
block capitals
to collect
to complete (a form)
computer games
(to go) dancing
date of birth
details
driving
to enjoy
to explain
free time
hill walking
(to go) horse riding
instruction
to be interested (in s.thing)
interesting
Internet
keep-fit exercises
notice
occupation
package
personal
to play
shop assistant
to sign (your name)
signature
to spell
to study
suggestion
to surf (the Internet)
surname
warning
watersports
windsurfing

Unit 1 Lesson 2
to accept
to agree
armchair
to attend
books
to brush
to check
climate
to comb
daily
to describe
desk
to dial
dishes
to dust
to feed
to forget
furniture
(a pair of) glasses
hair
to hand in
to imagine
international
interview
to invent
invention
to iron
to join in
make-up
medicine
meeting
message
mirror
to miss
mobile phone
to offer
palace
parcel
pet
philosopher
(what a) pity
to plug in
popular
to put away
to put on

to put up
radio
scientist
shirt
shoelaces
(a pair of) shoes
situation
soap
(a pair of) socks
to suggest
to take off
teeth
to thank
to tidy
to tie
to turn on
to turn up
umbrella
walkman
(to do the) washing-up
worried

Unit 2 Lesson 1
blackboard
boring
cakes
CD (compact disc)
to cook
correct
the cost (of s.thing)
document
(to send an) e-mail
enjoyable
equipment
favourite
to fry (an egg)
fun
to be good (at s.thing)
hobby
incorrect
ingredients
keyboard
to last
length
to look forward (to s.thing)
magazines
mouse
newspaper
to respond
screen
stuff
textbook
useful
video cassette
video player
videotape

Unit 2 Lesson 2
adult
adventure story
to advertise
amusing
autobiography
to belong (to s.body)
biography
bookshop
to borrow
to take care
charming
to create
cruel
damage
danger
daughter
deadly
delighted
design
dinosaur
to disappear
to discover
distant

to encourage
enemy
excitement
exciting
film star
gossip
grandson
to guide
to happen
heavy
hero
horror
humour
to hunt (for s.thing)
(a police) inspector
to investigate
to invite
journey
kind
to lend
to look for
to manage (to do s.thing)
marvellous
murder
mystery
old-fashioned
opinion
to pass (time)
planet
powerful
to prepare
to prove
to publish
realistic
to recognize
to request
to respect
romance
science fiction
secret
shadow
to shoot
spaceship
space travel
a spoonful (of s.thing)
stage
to steal
stormy
strange
successful
suitable
surprise
teenager
thriller
universe
victim
visitor
to win
wise

Unit 3 Lesson 1
accommodation
answerphone
arrangements
available
belongings
booking
brochure
cabin
(to go) camping
campsite
credit card
deck
destination
to discuss
downstairs
employee
excursion
experience
expert
facilities
flow

guest house
guidebook
handicrafts
hotel
inexperienced
level
luggage
map
market
minimum
nervous
nightlife
official
to pack
package holiday
passenger
penguin
photographs
(to have a) picnic
postcards
preparation
to prevent
to put up
(to make a) reservation
to run out (of s.thing)
scenery
scuba-diving
shark
shells
shower
sightseeing
souvenirs
(to go) sunbathing
(a pair of) sunglasses
suntan lotion
to supply
tour
travel agency
trip
unattended
value
variety
vehicle
volcano
wallet
whale
wildlife

Unit 3 Lesson 2
to accompany
advertisement
appearance
application form
to apply (for a job)
architect
artist
bank clerk
biologist
businessman/woman
chemist
choice
to decide
decision
doctor
to earn (a salary)
to employ
employment
engineer
to fill in (a form)
fortunately
to get up
to govern
government
hard work
insurance
journalist
lawyer
lift
lucky
manager
microscope
musician

to organize
physicist
to pick (s.one) up
police officer
profession
qualification
recording studio
responsible
to retire
retirement
rules
satisfactory
staff
stressful
strike
to succeed
success
traffic
typical
unfamiliar
uniform
unsuitable
unusual
vegetarian

Unit 4 Lesson 1
balcony
basement
bath
bathroom
bedroom
bedside table
blanket
blinds
block of flats
calculator
chest of drawers
coffee table
cooker
curtains
cushions
dining room
dishwasher
dressing table
fridge
garage
garden
hairdryer
hallway
kitchen
lamp
living room
mirror
packed lunch
pillows
to remember
seaside
shampoo
sheet
sink
sofa
stairs
storeroom
towel (rail)
vase
wardrobe
washbasin
waterproof
wood

Unit 4 Lesson 2
to advise
amount
amusing
anxious
attitude
attractive
blond(e)
bored
boring
careful
careless
celebration
cheerful

to compare
to complain
confident
to correspond
curly
to develop
development
dull
education
fair
foolish
funny
hard-working
high school
honest
intelligence
lazy
to measure
middle-aged
miserable
to point
pretty
professor
psychologist
to recommend
serious
shy
slim
smart
to smile
speed
strong
tired
truthful
ugly
understanding
university
weak

Unit 5 Lesson 1
admission
to arrange
art gallery
attraction
breakage
changing rooms
to climb
collection
department store
discount
display
entrance (fee)
to exhibit
giftshop
to hire
home-made
in advance
to inform
items
leaflet
mainland
pleasant
plenty
public
reasonable
to receive
refreshments
representative
to reserve
ruin
sports centre
surrounding
to touch
traditional
view
weigh
well-known

Unit 5 Lesson 2
appointment
arrival
attendant
bank account
boarding pass

carriage
to catch
to check in
to check out (of)
convenient
to cross out
to disturb
to draw out
driver
explanation
fare
to fill in (a form)
forename
furnished
gate
to get in
to get off
to get on
to give in
to hurry up
instead of
to land
to lend
license
luggage
meter
passenger
personal
pilot
platform
position
report
station
stop
to switch on
to take off
ticket
timetable
to turn over
underground

Unit 6 Lesson 1
acceptance
bargain
belt
boot
buttons
charge
cheque
clothing
collar
cotton
department
electrical
escalator
example
fashion
fashionable
goods
invitation
lift
out of order
paragraph
pocket
reason
receipt
receive
reduce
refusal
repair
sale
shopping centre
silk
skirt
sleeve
speciality
to spend
spices
spots
stall
street market
stripes
sweater
tie
(a pair of) tights
tip
to try on
topic

upstairs
vegetables
wool
zip

Unit 6 Lesson 2
advantage
convenient
crowded
dangerous
dirty
employment
entertainment
forest
fresh air
inconvenient
lonely
noisy
objects
peaceful
polluted
relaxing
rice
safe
spoon
stressful
sunny
traffic
transport
vehicle
way (of life)

Unit 7 Lesson 1
to add
bananas
beans
beef
burgers
butter
carrots
cheese
chicken
duck
fork
garlic
grapes
hard-boiled egg
herbs
impressive
knife
lamb
mayonnaise
to mix (together)
mixing bowl
mixture
mushrooms
olives
onions
oranges
owl
peas
pepper
plums
potato
to pour
recipe
salt
sausages
seeds
selection
sharp
snack
a spoonful (of
s.thing)
steak
tasty
tomatoes
tomato sauce
triangle
tuna fish

Unit 7 Lesson 2
to afford
to allow
to annoy
argument
average
to blame

circumstances
cupboard
divide
dizzy
early
to expect
fancy
to find
to fit
fussy
knock
to lead to
likely
lucky
to mind
miserable
to operate
opinion
privacy
regret
relationship
to repair
to review
selfish
to separate
to share
shelf
storage
tidiness
to tidy up
wardrobe

Unit 8 Lesson 1
according to
bat
to be born
bear
to beat
bee
to breathe
brilliant
to bury
changeable
cheerful
chest
clear
clouds
coal
coast
cool
countryside
cow
creature
damp
deaf
to defend
depressed
to destroy
to dig up
disease
dolphin
to dry up
dull
dusty
elephant
encouraging
environment
extraordinary
extremely
to fall down
fields
to fight
fine
to fly
foggy
forecast
freezing
frost
gold
goldfish
gorilla
height
horse
human
hunger
inhabitants
iron
jump

kick
kitten
lightning
to measure
minerals
mist
monkey
mouse
nature
to overtake
owner
pavement
pet
to pick
to pollute
to pour
poverty
to prevent
rabbit
rain
to reach
to realize
to rescue
rubbish
search
seldom
to set out
shower
snake
snow
spider
to spoil
storms
to strike
to suffer
sunshine
to tear
thunder
tiger
tongue
urgent
warm
to watch
weather
to weigh
wind

Unit 8 Lesson 2
to admire
beach
border
to break (down)
bush
camel
canal
canoe
cave
cliff
climb
continent
to cross
desert
director
distance
district
eagle
edge
to float
to flood
foreign
frontier
to hang
hole
interval
irrigation
island
jungle
local
location
mountain
mud
nest
on foot
on horseback
passport
path
project
to promise

to provide
restful
rock
row
ruins
sand
scenery
to set (the video)
shade
to shine
shore
to smell
soil
speed
stream
temperature
to tour
track
villain
waterfall
wave
website

Unit 9 Lesson 1
adventurer
to attend
balloon
baseball
to brush
circus
clown
crab
to discover
driving test
entertainment
envelope
facts
to fail
to feed
flower
frightened
golf
ground
gymnastics
hammer
handle
hockey
to introduce
to invent
judo
juggling
nails
needle
net
notepaper
paint
pins
poetry
pot
to present
racket
refreshing
safety (rules)
sailing
scissors
seeds
skiing
skill
to slide
spade
stamp
table tennis
to take up
training
tunnel
watering can
windsurfing
workshop

Unit 9 Lesson 2
accident
to ache
ambulance
aspirin
benefit
blood
to consider
to cure

deaf
deep
dentist
disease
documentary
to fall over
flu
Get well!
grateful
healthy
hearing (aid)
hospital
hurt
jogging
lifestyle
to look (after)
opportunity
patient
sickness
sore throat
stress
to take care (of)
toothache
unhealthy
valuable

Unit 10 Lesson 1
action (film)
actor
audience
backing (group)
camera
channel
characters
chat room
to clap
clubbing
to come up
comedian
commercial
crew
curtain
dancer
delicious
director
disc jockey
drummer
film critic
interval
interviewer
lead (singer)
lines
performance
pianist
play
plot
pop group
to practise
presenter
programme
region
reviews
screen
series
singer
soap opera
(to be) sold out
stage
studio
violinist
wet

Unit 10 Lesson 2
communication
confused
to contact
face-to-face
fax
letters
misunderstanding
to pay attention
to phone
recent
relaxed
respect (for)
screen
skills
word-processing